SKINNY WEE LEGS

By Damien G C Devaney

First Published by Amazon 2012

Autobiographical Humour

SKINNY WEE LEGS

By Damien G C Devaney

Dedicated to:

My little sister Yvonne who died at the age of only thirty-three years leaving two little boys who simply did not know what had happened to them. When she was just three years of age the old clock chimed and she sang a rhyme to it that went like this:

Wee Wong, ding dong,
Ding dong, wee Wong.

After that her elder brothers gave her the little pet name of 'Wee Wong'

After Wee Wong died my wife paid her the greatest compliment any woman could pay to another:
'You know, I often wished I had been Yvonne'

Accreditation: My thanks to Joe and Wilma Clint for some precious photographs

LIST OF CONTENTS

SKINNY WEE LEGS

Preface

My little grandfather, Patrick Joseph Devaney was a bastard. Not in the sense of today's meaning of the word, but in the true meaning: a totally innocent little child born out of wedlock. The Church, the State and a certain 'Matilda Kerr' spread a passionate hatred of such unfortunate human beings, treating them as 'animals of the field.'

How such treatment could possibly be justified is simply beyond comprehension. As the perpetrators of this injustice proudly walked into church to worship their god they did not give a second thought to the fact that their vile tongues of hatred created the only evil associated with the quantum-physical equation of
conception. In those days of the dark shadows of the mind, a combination of class distinction, prejudice and outright brainwashing ensured that the sons and daughters would carry the wounds caused by the sins of the fathers.

On finding out that Patrick Joseph Devaney was a bastard, Matilda Kerr (as Matilda Gilmore) forbade her daughter, Eliza Anne (Lizanne) from ever seeing again the boy she had fallen in love with. But, Lizanne's brother, Francis, was to die at the age of twenty-one and his dying wish was: 'Please let Lizanne marry Patrick.'

Francis was the 'apple of his Matilda's eye' and she reluctantly granted his wish. She did not promise to treat Patrick in any other way than that of being a

bastard and this she did. Patrick was a steward at sea and from one trip, during the second world war, he simply did not return. I have written evidence to show how great a love that man had for his two little boys and that would tend to argue against desertion.

From the family's point of view Patrick Joseph was 'lost on a convoy' but his papers could not be traced as he always sailed under an assumed name as there was no 'births for Catholics' on most ships sailing from Ireland or Scotland in those days of sectarianism. Day in and day out; his two little sons searched the horizon for a ship that just might bring their father back and this has lead me to write and include my
Poem 'Skinny Wee Legs'

SKINNY WEE LEGS

My father also went to sea but one day as he was coming off his ship in a Liverpool Dock he saw an old man gazing intensely at him. My father walked away but turned around to witness the old man still gazing at him. He did not go back even though he truly
believed he had seen his old father - alive.

SKINNY WEE LEGS

"Dee!" A man hailed from a crowed table in a well known loyalist pub on the outskirts of Belfast.
"Oh, my god! I hope that's not me, he's shouting at," I trembled, for being a catholic found in a loyalist pub, in Belfast, in the 1980's spelt imminent danger. Being in the wrong place, at the wrong time in that city has even resulted in an early grave for many innocent people. I had taken the chance, in going there, to meet a prospective business colleague as it was one of the few places we had common knowledge of.

The shouting continued: "Dee! Dee! Come over here ya fucking auld bastard."
"My god, it must be me; nobody else is moving!" I considered slipping out of the door but that would only raise suspicion and get me into deeper trouble.
I gingerly turned around. It was the worst possible scenario; the man doing the shouting was looking at me. His three companions looked like wartime Ukrainian, concentration-camp capos: thick set, shaven headed and with steroid-induced, bulging biceps adorned with union jacks, Ulster flags and the unmistakable letters 'UDA'

and 'UFF' (Ulster Defence Association and Ulster Freedom Fighters – the latter being a 'front-up name' for a branch of the former, involved in assassinations, murder and grievous bodily harm.)
I admit now that the first words that came to my mind were: "Is this my last day on earth? Will anyone ever find my body?"

The man who had done the shouting beckoned me over. Suddenly I recognised him. He was one of the two little protestant boys who had been in our little gang as children – Harry or 'Muddle' as was his gang name in those days of long, long ago.
"Come over here, ya auld bastard! Boys this is Dee – our leader."

Had he called me by my true Christian name – I was as good as dead, for in that province names can be your death warrant. After the plantation of Ulster by mainly Scottish Presbyterian Covenanters in the seventeenth century that religious body had a problem with Christian names, having denounced anything remotely connected with papists they were opposed to calling their offspring any name associated with catholic saints. This restricted their choice to Old Testament names and the use of surnames as Christian names. Quite simply, if a man was called Wilson Crawford he was deemed to be a protestant and in contrast: a man called Malachy O'Rourke was deemed to be a catholic. Often a man's driving license has sent him as a corpse to some remote beach or mountain wilderness.

Harry had progressed to a high position within that loyalist, paramilitary organization, the UDA and to introduce me as 'Our Leader' commanded immediate respect. There were smiles and grunts of acknowledgement as the brutal looking foot-soldiers grabbed my hand in turn. I remember thinking silly things, such as: "My hand feels like a toy" as they squeezed the living day-lights out of it as each tried to prove to me, he was stronger than the last one.
As Harry called for a drink for me, I realized that he was playing a game. He was showing that little boss of long, long ago who was the big boss now.
"I wish to god, I hadn't hit him across the ass with a hurly stick when he overstepped the mark all those years back. Would he remember? Would I hear the dreaded words: "Come on, we will go somewhere quieter for a drink'?"

It was then I spied my future business partner appearing in the doorway: "Sorry lads, must go, that's my boss over there."
I arose and there was more hand-shakes and heavy back thumping as I made my way to the door.
I nudged my future business partner outside.
"Nice company," he mused.
"What are you driving?"
"Beamer 530, why?"
"Just get me out of here as fast as you can."

Coming from this part of Ireland, I, like all, residing here, am exposed to hatred in the form of bigotry. The English now understanding this more clearly as they are faced by a growing conflict between Christianity and Islam. The Muslim extremists carry placards calling for the beheading of those insulting Islam whilst the extreme Christians burn copies of the Koran. This lust for vengeance is a singularity of evil irrespective of its being; Catholic v Protestants (here in N. Ireland), Tamil v Sinhalese, Jew v Muslim, Hutu v Tutsi or the Arabian Batahin v the African Kuku in Sudan. The Elohim (the Great Spirits of eternal advancement) do not distinguish between ethnic, religious or tribal causes; they simply see it as 'hatred' – a feeling human beings seem to be quite at ease with in matters that are of personal interest to them; hence neo, right-wing, self-serving, political exploitation since time immemorial. People who harbor this hatred will take it with them to the next existence and will have no interest in progressing to the Heavens – where everyone resides in harmony, peace, kindness and love. The aforesaid people will wait in Limbo for their return to this material existence where they again can experience their feeling of hatred; ironically, in most cases in opposite ethnic, religious or tribal circumstances to their previous sojourn here.

I have witnessed the result of hatred in my home country and I although I was caught up in Belfast in the mass bombing on the so-called Bloody Friday, it has not had such a deep effect on me as the sight of a long street of burning homes in a place called Farrington Gardens. I have since associated the smell of burning furniture with sectarian hatred.

But it is not my intention to delve too deeply into such matters in this little book but anyone interested in transcendental exploration should read my other book: 'I am Memory' published by CreateSpace, as is this one (subsidiary of

Amazon.com) with the ISBN 978-1440466120, but before I go back to 'Harry' I will relate a funny experience I recently encountered on a tube train in London: a Muslim, fully dressed in flowing white robes and with a little cotton pill-box, cap sat down in front of me, took out his Koran and started reading it sometimes orally expressing his devotion in the recitation of some passages. The train stopped at a station and an Englishman jumped aboard and sat beside me and opposite to the Islamic gentleman.
When he spied the devout Muslim; his eyes widened; his mouth fell open and he shouted: "Holy fuck," as he jumped to his feet and fled out of the closing door.
My mate turned to me and asked: "What was that all about?"
"Sounded like someone has just remembered he should have been making love with his friendly vicar," I responded.

Long, long ago, when we were little children, Harry was referred as 'Muddle'. Someone had given him a greyhound that had been rejected by a trainer since it preferred running around in ever tightening circles until it was in danger of disappearing up its own ass. On the few occasions, he ran straight there was no dog in the neighbour-

hood that could keep up with him. He often slowed down, looked his pursuer in the eye then took off again as if to say: “This is easy.”
One day he (Muddle – not the dog) had an idea, although, as you are about to find out, the dog would have had more sense.
“I’ve got my daddy’s matches here to light a wee fire to warm up our hands,” Muddle confided in me.
Just one of the reasons that this was not a good idea was: it was in the middle of summer, and the second reason was; the grass and shrubs were tinder dry. We chose a wild patch of ground, known as the ‘Warren’ that lay next to the sands of Cloughey Bay. We lit a couple of little fires then pretended to be the fire-brigade and stamped them out.
“Fire-brigades put fires out with water,” Muddle informed me.
“We haven’t got a bucket!”
“We could just use our hands.”
“Couldn’t carry much in our hands,” I protested.
“I can carry a gallon.”

That persuaded me. We lit three or four little fires then headed off to the sea for a couple of handfuls of salt-water. The sea happened to be out and by the time we returned the fires had taken hold in an alarming fashion. Not to be deterred, we threw the water unto the blaze and hoped for some kind of miracle. After a pathetic little sizzling sound, we reverted back to the tried and tested method of stamping. This made little difference as, by that time, the small fires had linked up to form one big blazing ring and there was Muddle, Teke, Jap and myself – stuck in the middle of it.

"How will we get out?" Muddle panicked.

"We have to run through it quick," I instructed.

"We'll get burned."

"If you can't get out I'll get Mister Keene to ring up the fire-brigade." (Mister Keene was the only person in the village with a telephone).

It failed to strike me that the fire-brigade was stationed six miles away in the little town of Portaferry and by the time it arrived; Muddle would have much resembled a barbequed sausage. I made a dash through the flames and luckily; my little play-mate followed close behind.

We charged off, for the safety of our homes, which were only a few hundred yards away. Rather unfortunately for us, it was the height of the tourist season and it was just a matter of yards before we bumped into a family sunning themselves. Nineteen-forty-seven was one of our

hottest summers but, even allowing for that fact; they still must have wondered why the temperature began climbing at such an alarming rate.
It was then that Muddle sunk us: "Look Mister, there's a big fire up on that bank and we didn't start it."
He dragged his grubby, little pockets inside out: "See! We haven't got any matches."
The man and his wife glared suspiciously at four little boys with singed hair, singed eyebrows and smelling like smoked herrings on a fishmonger's hook.
Further down the shore I took Muddle by the shoulders and told him: "Listen to me now! We didn't start that big fire. It must have been them tourists but we nearly got burned trying to put it out."
When the best part of five acres was burned to cinders the fire-brigade finally arrived. They were followed later by Constable Milligan, a comely old gentleman, who accepted my mother's explanation for my kippered appearance as: "Helping to put out a fire some tourists started."
That didn't prevent me getting a severe hiding from my mother – a woman known locally as 'The Targe'.

Although our father was a first lieutenant in the Royal Navy at that time cash was not so plentiful that it might be handed out in the form of pocket-money. This meant that my little brothers and I were always on the prowl for discarded lemon-ade-bottles that could be sold back in Mister Keene's shop for tuppence and later a treepenny-bit. The Warren was the best place to find lemon-ade bottles and not only lemonade bottles but money as well.

According to a theory of my brother Patrick (better known in those days as 'Teke'); "When men go over the Warren with women, they some-times have to pull their trousers down if it gets too warm. That is when money falls out of their pockets."

That theory was enhanced by the other little prot-estant member of our gang; Josiah Flint (we just called him 'Flint') who informed us that if a woman and a man were lying amongst the sand dunes; if you stood there long enough watching them the man might give you some money to go away and get some sweets.

That sounded great to me, so I asked: "Do they always give you money for sweets?"

"No! Sometimes they just shout at you: "Fuck off you - over there! I can see you!"

One of my earliest childhood memories is of the 'Tammany Nominee Band.' In New York, in the nineteenth-century the Democratic Party opened its headquarters in Tammany Hall. The police and most of the politicians were in the hands of the Mafia and there was little chance of a nomination without those gangsters' approval; thus, a Tammany Nominee was considered to be the most corrupt thing imaginable. My father must have been knowledgeable in that field for it was he who chose to name our little dangling bit 'Tammany Nominee.' Other kids had 'Niggs, Prats, Pricks' and even 'Pinkers' but we had to have 'Tammany Nominee.' In the nineteen-forties, in most country homes, bath night happened only once a week and it occurred on a Saturday. A long, narrow, zinc coated, steel bath, called a bungalow-bath, was unhitched from its hanging hook, in the outhouse, brought into the kitchen and filled with warm water. A lump of carbolic soap was thrown in and, in the case of our house, three dirty kids followed in a similar fashion.

On the evening in question, we three children were left to dry ourselves in front of the open fire whilst our mother went into the 'big room' to sort out some underwear for us. Our underwear was made from bleached flour-bags as was everything else in our home from sheets to babies' bonnets. Kirkistown Orange Hall Pipe Band just happened to be passing our house at that particular moment and, of course, drew our attention. Mother returned to find that her three little boys had vanished. She looked out of the window and there they were: attached unto the end of Kirkistown Orange Hall Pipe Band, saucepan lids, clanging together as cymbals with Tammany Nominees swinging gently two and fro in perfect harmony.

"Suffering Jesus, would you believe that? What in the name of Christ am I to do?" she groaned. She said it was the most humiliating thing she ever had to do: "All of them protestant folk, in all their grandeur, marching behind them ones with their kilts and their pipes and three wee, catholic, bare arses bringing up the rear and I had to go out there, like a bloody egit (Irish way of saying idiot) and trail you all in." The Cherokee children asses would have looked pale compared to ours by the time the Targe has finished with them.

A week or so later, Mother's friend, Lilly Gibson, arrived in with a big smile on her face:

"Did you hear the latest, Peg?" she laughed.

"What now, Lilly?"

"Bobby Browns cows went down the Quarter Brea just ahead of the Kirkistown Pipe Band and they covered the road in shit and the band-men were slipping and slithering all over the place. Jesus, Peg, there were some notes squeezed out of them auld bags that no one had ever heard in their life before. I heard some of the Orangemen were blaming your wanes."
"Kiss my arse, Lily," the Targe responded.

As a little lad I often took refuge, from the thundering voice of my mother, in a neighbouring garden, which was overgrown with wild flowers and weeds which grew to a massive height. Well, when you only measure three feet yourself, everything around you looks a bit on the big side. In my little haven of solitude, I reigned supreme. For some reason, I associated my mother with thunder. I think it had something to do with the dark night when we had to walk home through a thunder-storm. My two younger brothers were pushed in a pram by our mother, whilst I walked alongside holding on for grim death. Sheet lightning, from directly overhead, lit the whole countryside up whilst fork lightning streaked through the sky out over the Irish Sea. The thunder was deafening but between bursts I was aware of mother's prayers: "Jesus, Mary and Saint Joseph save us this night. Holly Souls pray for us." She was quite hysterical.

But back to my haven: by pushing an old wooden barrel through the weeds in the neighbour's garden, I formed a sort of maze. I flattened an area in the centre of the garden where I laid smelly old hemp sacks to protect me from stingy nettles, prickly thistles and a least some of the creepy-crawlies. I raised the weeds up again at the entrance the tunnel to my little haven to conceal it from Mother who in addition to her, many gifts of detection had the instinctive scenting powers of a blood-hound. The pilots in the war-planes that constantly flew above could be forgiven for believing they had seen a crop circle down below.

The first indication that 'The Targe' (my mother) was 'on the war-path' was the snapping open of the big door latch. That was followed by the bull-dozing aside of everything that lay in her path; then the opening and slamming of outhouse doors, the clanging and clattering of any old junk that might just conceal somebody trying to escape his daily chores. As she searched in vain, her tirade of threats, insults and swearing had a very un-nerving effect on me and often when my courage didn't hold, I make a mad dash for the emergency exit that led out behind the neighbour's old pump-house. One day, in particular, she caught me crouching behind the rusty old pump.

"What the hell are you doing there you skiving, bloody gob-shite (corruption of the Irish 'gairbhseach' meaning rough or ruffian)" she roared.

"Eh! Eh, getting some water for the house."

"And what in hell's blazes were you going to use as a bucket?"

On the days she didn't flush me out I learned lessons in my haven; lessons that I would not forget for the rest of my life. I watched industrious midges, ants and bees working communally, flies and many insects working individually if not in direct competition and the mighty assassins – the spiders- delivering death. It greatly perturbed me to see that they were cannibalistic and it made me think of Mad Mick, a mentally disturbed man who roamed the countryside harassing everyone he met – forcing his way into people's homes and demanding food. Big Ernie told me that Mad Mick was a cannibal and that he had seen him throwing human bones into the sea off Charlie's Rocks.

"Do you think he was making soup out of people?" I enquired.
"Nay! I think he just eats people raw."
"Are you not afraid of Mad Mick?"
He screwed up his face, shook his head and said;
"Big Ernie's afraid of nobody."
Big Ernie earned a great deal of respect in our neighbourhood.

The most valuable lesson I learned from my childhood haven was that consciousness is not dependent upon the physical body. How it came about is this; I had become very relaxed as I observed the little creatures around me, and crossed the threshold of tranquillity and found the centre of my consciousness to be a few inches above and in front of my head. That is where I was seeing from and that is where I was thinking from. Of course, I panicked for I believed my spirit was about to drift off over 'Molly's Hills' and I would never be able to return to my family. No sooner had the panic set in than my consciousness returned to within my head.
Shortly after I emerged from my secret haven, I heard a roaring voice: "Where were you hiding?"
"In the …in the garden."

"No you bloody well were not, for I looked all over the place for you," the Targe screamed, clouting my lug-hole as I ran past her.

About sixteen years later I stood in the dock of a mock up magistrate's court and that experience came back to me when an inspector of police put that very same question to me: "Where were you hiding?'"

I had joined the Lancashire Constabulary during the winter of 1962 after an almighty row with my mother after which I simply had to get out of the house. I had not the remotest intention of making a career out of the move and treated the whole experience as some kind of a joke. This could be borne out by the amount of 'jankers' I served during my training for offences ranging from slovenliness whilst on parade to insubordination. To the best of my knowledge, the record stands to this very day. Initially, I was based at a police training school called Stanley Grange. I had arrived there six weeks ahead of the rest of the intake and had been given the job of lighting the fires, each day, in the police houses that were temporarily unoccupied. A uniformed batch of recruits was going through basic training and one of the exercises they had to carry out involved a break-in at a garage. Generally, there was nothing more to it than opening the classroom door and letting them descend upon the scene of the crime where they would search for previously planted clues – a more sophisticated version of ‘Hide the Parcel’ if you like. The raw recruits would then return to another classroom suitably converted into a police station or bridewell as the old hands liked to call it wherein they would sift through their evidence in front of the camp commandant and other lower ranking officers.

There was little or no excitement involved so I decided to spice things up a bit. I cut up newspapers, which I was supposed to light the fires with, into the size of five-pound notes; I got a marker and wrote on each ‘£5’ and stuffed them into my boiler-suit pocket, armed myself with a poker and lay in wait in the mock-up garage. The minute the recruits sighted the garage I took off like a bat out of hell, jumping shrubs, gates, barbed-wire fences and any other obstacle that got in the way. By the time I had opened up a couple of hundred yards on my pursuers the fatties began to drop out. After half a mile or so the fitter ones began to catch me, so I turned around, raised my hands in the air and uttered those infamous words: “It’s a fair cop.”

All the rules of arrest went out of the door as they rugby-tackled me into the mud, sat on my chest, stood on my legs and applied the handcuffs. There were at least six others eager young PCs struggling to claim the honour of putting their handcuffs on me.

"Thank you, but one pair of cuff will suffice, you never see a criminal being stuffed into the Black Maria with a dozen pairs of handcuffs on – did you?" I protested.

"Hi, we haven't got a police van to convey the prisoner to the police station," one enterprising young bobby reminded.

"March the bastard back," growled a thick-set man with a Glasgow accent.

"I will inform you - my parents went through a marriage service in 1938."

"Shut your gob!" the same voice shouted.

"Is that a formal caution or what?" I enquired.

I thought the Jock boy was going to hit me but another recruit stepped forward and administered half the caution before grinding to a halt and having to be helped out by a more studious looking young officer.

"You got that caution wrong I protested, therefore, legally you must set me free."

Jock shoved his boxer-nose up against mine: "So what is the right way, smart ass?"

"You are not obliged to do anything but anything you may do, will be lifted on a shovel and thrown in your face."
Jock walked away muttering: "Someone better stop me before I baton that Irish bastard."

"You lot forgot to search me!"
"I took the house breaking implement of you, didn't I?" a well built young recruit answered.
"My poker you mean? What if I'm armed or in possession of a gob-stopper or something?" I suggested hoping that someone would find the fake fivers.
"What's a gob-stopper," someone asked.
"It's a great big sweetie the size of your gob," the man from Glasgow informed him.
"He's right though, we must submit him to a full body search," the more intelligent one agreed.
"I object to being body searched."
"On what grounds?" the intelligent one seemed to have taken charge.
"I have been circumcised!"
"So what's that got to do with it?"
"The Rabbi who carried it out was suffering from a hang-over. It's a bit messy."
"The bastard is having you on." Jock intervened.
That was it: hands were suddenly all over me like a swarm of locusts on a treasure-hunt, until some-

body shouted excitingly: “Look! Look what I’ve just found! “What do you call this young man?” He shoved the cut paper in my face.
“Looks like the Lancashire Evening Post to me!” I muttered nonchalantly.
“Well it appears to me to be legal tender.”
“Your banker has his work cut out with you.”
“Never mind, you are under arrest for the criminal offence of aggravated burglary.”
“Not guilty; Officer!”

The fatties had by this time arrived on the scene and it was they, more than anyone, who roughly frog-marched me into the mock-bridewell where the acting duty sergeant’s eyes widened in disbelief.
“I arrested this man for the offence of aggravated burglary,” asserted the intelligent recruit from behind the fatties.
Sergeant Bell, a man with 15 years service was momentarily speechless.
Eventually, he stuttered: “You what?”
The arresting officer repeated his charge.
The big sergeant cleared his throat: “Would someone nip over to the office and ask inspector Carney would he come over and see me.”
Silence rained until the messenger returned with a white-haired inspector. He looked a bit absent

minded to me. Sergeant Bell and he conferred for a few moments after which the former announced that he would grant me bail to return to the same spot after lunch.
"The bastard should have been locked up," the Glaswegian grumbled.

I only found out years later when I spoke to Sergeant Bell at Widnes Police Station, what follows. After the surprised sergeant had gone through the actions of bailing me, he and the inspector had relayed the situation to the chief inspector who in turn informed Superintendent Butterworth the commandant of the training establishment. Between them, they decided that the opportunity was too good to miss so they hastily constructed a court-room in another building and six high-ranking officers sat officially as observers but unofficially as jurors with the commandant presiding in the biggest play-acting Stanley Grange had ever seen. An inspector by the name of DeBrooke, who was remarkably like Adolph Hitler but with a David Niven moustache, was chosen to prosecute and Carney, the old grey haled inspector defended.
After a handpicked few recruits gave evidence against me, it was the turn of the defence to take the stand. I was called to the witness box.

At the end of the usual swearing-in I was asked:
"What is your profession?"
"I'm a fire lighter – not to be confused with an arsonist, if I may add."
"I wish you wouldn't," old Butterworth sighed.
"Deport him back to Ireland," the Glaswegian shouted out.
"Eat your sweaty jock-strap," I retorted
"Have that man removed from the court," the acting judge demanded.
One of the eager fatties grabbed me by the arm.
"No, not the defendant; that man over there with the Scottish accent."
Sergeant Bell took the thick-set Scot by the arm and walked him out of the makeshift court.

"As a fire-fighter would you…"
"He's not a fire fighter man! He has just told the court, he is a fire lighter," the judge interrupted.
"I'm so sorry; I misheard what the man said."
Then turning towards me old Carney continued,
"Would I be correct in thinking a poker is essential to your profession?"
"It is very handy, Sir; it saves you burning your index finger."
"Please refrain from adding your personal comments," Butterworth interrupted me.

The old inspector leafed through his notes: "Oh yes, would you please tell the court why you were in possession of cut up newspapers?"
"It was the Lancashire Evening Post to be precise; I would have preferred the Liverpool Echo as it is more flammable – to light the fires you see!"
"No more questions," the old grey haired man sat down.
Inspector DeBrooke got to his feet: "Mister Fire Lighter, if I may presume to be so bold …" he spoke with a sort of whine, for it was rumoured that had he been around in the days of the Pied Piper of Hamlin that character would have been out of a job for DeBrooke's voice was said to have sickened rats.
"Mister Fire Lighter, where were you hiding? Where were you hiding when the police patrol disturbed you?"
"In the garden … err … I wasn't; I wasn't really hiding, Mine Feuer err … sorry, Sir."
"Young man! Young man, pull yourself together," the superintendent intervened.
"Sorry! Sorry, Sir" I answered pulling a pretend zip up to assure him I had got his message.
"You will take these proceedings seriously or find yourself facing disciplinary charges," the commandant warned me.

"Yes Sir! Indeed, Sir!"

The prosecuting inspector, who had given way to his superior officer, got to his feet again and continued the questioning: "If you were innocent of any wrong-doing; why did you run off?"
"They frightened me; they were shouting things like 'STOP THIEF', you know the sort of thing you would read in the Dandy or the Beano."
"Who was shouting such things?"
"The fatties, Sir. That's all they could do Sir, 'cause they had no hope of catching me."
"By the fatties you mean the overweight police recruits?"
"Mister DeBrooke! Mister DeBrooke," Butterworth protested.
DeBrooke wiped his brow, "I'm so sorry Sir."
He cleared his throat and resumed: "Did you run off and continue running until you were apprehended by several officers?"
"Apprehended!" I shook my head, "It was more like a free-for-all in Argyle Street in Glasgow at throwing out time."
"When you were 'APPREHENDED' did you not admit your guilt by saying: "It's a fair cop?"
"But he was fair; look, him over there! Well, perhaps he is more sandy than fair, now that I have time to study him more thoroughly."

"Thank you! Thank You! Now explain to the court why you had a substantial amount of pieces of paper in your pocket each marked with the number 5 and bearing the pound Sterling sign."
"So that I could bluff that bunch there that they were real five-pound notes."
"And why should you do that?"
"So that I could make them look daft."
"And you appear to have succeeded in doing so to a greater extent than even you anticipated," Superintendent Butterworth interjected: "Now Mister Carney, if I was in your shoes, I would be seeking a verdict of 'No case to answer'.

Inspector Carney got to his feet: "I submit M'Lud that my client has no case to answer.
The commandant acknowledged: "I agree; this case is dismissed. The accused is free to leave this court."
Pandemonium broke out with recruits shouting and thumping tables. Sergeant Bell produced his pocket-book and threatened to take names for disciplinary proceedings if the revolt did not die down. Jock from Glasgow whispered in my ear:
"Look what you've done. Argyle Street was never as bad as this." We became quite close friends from then until we received our postings. I did not hear from him after that but I have to

add: most of the fatties didn't last a year on the streets.

There is a golf course close to the house in which I was born and although we were forbidden to play on it, it was one of our favourite haunts as children. The second and tenth greens are perched high on grassy mounds beside even higher grassy knolls – ideal hiding places for scruffy little kids that have been up to no good. An approaching golfer, to the tenth green, for example, is blind to where his ball comes to rest as the green is at least twenty feet higher than the fairway from where he plays his stroke. Our little gang (the infamous five might be appropriate) would lie flat on the green to keep out of sight and gently roll a ball or two back down the slope:
"Oh, bad luck old boy!" opponents would try to suppress a titter.
"Goodness gracious, not another one!"
One day Flint overstepped the mark and rolled a third ball back down the slope.
"Fuck me! There must be gusts of wind up there or are we putting too much back-spin on the ball?"
Hitting the ball in a straight line was as much as that particular party could do – never mind putting on back-spin.

Another favourite trick was to retrieve a stray ball from the long grass and pop it in the hole:
"Oh jolly hockey sticks old boy!"
"Well, by the Good Lord! There are two of them in here! "Must be some sort of a record don't you think."
If the ground was soft, we often stood on a ball so that it was well and truly sunk into the grass. That caused some confusion and much referring to the rule book.
The best trick of all involved; lifting a golf ball from the green and scrambling up the higher knoll with it in a little trouser pocket that didn't have a hole in it. When it appeared that the golfers were about to give up searching one of us would throw the ball high in the air, landing it on the green as close to the hole as possible. Initially, the golfers thought it might be a stray ball from the club of Dangerous Barney but on inspection it proved to be the missing ball.
"Well bugger me! That took some time coming down," observed a man, previously thought to be rather good-living.

The eleventh fairway was the shortest hole on the course with the green being little more than a couple of hundred yards beyond our favourite tenth green. I took a ball from the last mentioned, green and plopped it in the cup on the eleventh green and managed to scramble back on top of the high grassy mound before the golfers appeared. After a failed search, they teed off at the eleventh.

"Good God! There's a ball in the hole," an amazed player showed it around for identification.

"It's mine! That's the ball I hit at the tenth," a golfer in a Fairisle jumper jumped around excitingly.

"You can't win this hole with a shot from the last one," shouted another player.

"It's in the hole, isn't it?"

"Yes, but the wrong bloody hole!"

"It was some shot to have carried this distance."

"Wrong club, perhaps!" tittered the man with the big belly who had to have his clubs shortened so that he could swing from underneath his protrusion.

The debate raged on until we could hear them no more.

We didn't always get away with our little pranks. One day Teke crawled around on his knees balancing a greens-flag down Muddle's trouser-belt. He was also crawling around the putting green.

"What in the name of hell's blazes is going on up there," an approaching golfer moaned? Unknown to us; it wasn't a two-ball game; it was a three-ball game for the third golfer had hit his ball into the schoolmaster's garden which was blocked from our view. He came up almost behind us.

"What is going on up there then," his mate repeated.

"Don't rightly know, but there appears to be a wee fellow with a pole up his arse and another one is crawling around after him trying to pull it out."

"Hadn't you better go to their assistance?"

When we all ran off he growled: "What they need is something extra up their arses – my frigging toe!"

Sometimes we got as much fun watching golfers as we did getting up to our pranks. In later life I invented a game based on the predicaments of Dangerous Barney. On two occasions that I know of his ball finished behind from where he had played it. The first time he clattered it smack into the gable of the schoolmaster's house and his ball finished a good hundred yards behind where he stood. The ball was ripped to pieces yet he still played on with it but on the putting-green it bobbed about like a drunken Bombay runner and he finished up with a ten on his card, which, I would add was an average score for Barney. On the second occasion, he struck a ball from the hollow on the ninth, unto the previously described green on the knoll. There was a gale of wind blowing that day. He took a ten iron and his ball went up almost perpendicularly, was caught with a great gust and taken back over his head. I called my game 'Gusty Golf', but it didn't sell too well.

One day we saw a group of golfers gathered around a player who was lying on the grass. We went over and saw that a local man, Tommy Kyle, had a large round lump on his head and it was obvious he had been struck by a golf-ball.
"Did he swallow it?" enquired my younger brother whose gang name was Jap.
"Swallow what?" I asked.
"His golf-ball!"
"No! Somebody hit it into his gob," cut in the better-informed Flint.
Well, come to think about it – the bump was about the same size as a golf-ball.

That little episode, unfortunately having a bit of fun at the expense of the afflicted, came back to me donkey's years later as I sat at the computer teaching my six-year-old granddaughter, Holly how to drive a train. When constructing the rail-way-line she forgot to link the track. The result was her train crashed with the engine and carriages all rolling down an embankment.

She turned to me quite aghast: "What do I do now, Grandpa?"

"You are the driver of the train and it is your responsibility to take care of the passengers. Do you know what 'responsibility' means?"

"Yes, it means it's my job."

"Well you must go around the passengers and tell them to be calm and then tell them what they must do."

"Right! Everybody be calm," she started off.

"All them who are injured make your way to the hospital where you will get flowers and grapes. All them who are dead make your way to the graveyard where you will get buried."

Way back in the early nineteenth century, the Catholic Church ruled her Irish flock with a fist of iron where compassion was replaced with oppression. 'Illegitimacy' was the cardinal sin and our little family almost didn't happen because of it.

About the year 1875 an old man in dark robes whipped a wet, mud-splattered, scruffy, old pony, pulling a rickety old trap, through the driving rain. He muttered and sighed as the trap bumped from one pot-hole to the next. He would have sworn but he couldn't for he was a priest. That may not have put him off but the young girl holding a sodden shawl over her head was the real reason he didn't. It was a long way from the rough winding little lanes of Sligo to Belfast. There he had an appointment with the Ardrossan steamer; well, perhaps not so much he, as the young girl by his side. He would pick up a one-way ticket for her to Scotland from the offices of the steam-package company, Burns and Laird Line. She would not be returning; she had become an outcast:

"No need to sit there sniffling and crying. It's too late for crying. You made your bed and now you must lie in it," the man who had lived through the potato famine and the oppression of the Crown that decimated the population of Ireland, cast a pitiless, sideways glance at her.

Mary; my great-grandmother was a pretty little thing but little more than a child. Her little head was filled with confusion and dread but most of all it was filled with guilt for she was with child

and the man in black beside her, took every opportunity to remind her that she had mortally sinned against her maker and brought shame and disgrace upon her family:
"A shame and disgrace they will not recover from. Do you realize your father will never be able to hold his head up in the church ever again? You have destroyed your own family as if you had taken a gully-knife and cut their throats!"
The girl sobbed loudly as she remembered the shrieking of her mother as they parted for ever. She imagined a banshee would make that sound as it peered out, with red eyes, from dark plantations; warning of impending death. However, her mother has no say in the matter; she did what her husband bid and he, in turn, bowed to power absolute in the form of the parish priest and the puritanical brainwashing of those days.

It was the old priest who came up with the solution when he was informed that the child was pregnant: "Haven't your family, a relative or something in Glasgow?"
"She's only a distant relation and she lives in the Gorbals at that. No child should be asked to live in the Gorbals," Mary's mother lamely protested but the little girl's fate was sealed.

Within the hour, a dispatch to the 'old aunt in the Gorbals' was arranged and within the next few days the money was found for her ticket, with a little over and above, to get her by until she could be fixed up with a job in a dusty, cold flax-mill.

The old cleric knew he could change ponies in Augher and whilst he had a meal with the local parish priest, little Mary was ushered into the kitchen where the housekeeper dried out her clothes as well as she could in the time available and gave the child a bite to eat. As dawn broke the following day the domineering man in black protested bitterly as he had to wait at the Sand Quay, at the top of Belfast's Oxford Street for it was just his luck to get caught up in a herd of filthy bullocks that were being deliberately stampeded down to the Ardrossan steamer, a ship in which there was little difference in animal and third class (steerage) accommodation. Cow hands were thrashing at the frenzied animals causing them to slip and fall amongst their own flying dung. That, together with the bellowing and excruciating stench must have made the little girl think she was being transported to Bedlam.

And the word 'Bedlam' may fall short in describing the conditions of the Gorbals: Tenements, some three, four and sometimes five stories high blackened the skyline. Generally, the higher stories were accessed by an enclosed stairwell tower, which stood in front of the block like a castle keep. Over the years, they became filthy with rubbish and excrement and were a major cause in spreading disease. Worse were the towering unprotected stone steps that soared high to the upper stories of the more ancient buildings. God knows how many drunks met their death by falling from those slippery steps and it is said that at least one person died for every stone that paved the district. I could well believe it. The slum housed immigrants from both Ireland and Italy and oppressed Jews from other parts who came to seek employment in the local mills and dockyards. It was not a great mix for peaceful communal living. Little Mary simply would not be able to understand life beyond the leafy lanes and rolling seas of the coast of Sligo.

Having secured the pony to a convenient hitching post the old priest hung a nose bag over the animal's head and then disappeared into the booking office. Half an hour later he emerged from an adjacent pub, lifted the little girl from the trap and carelessly planted her small clogged-feet in the filth of the cobbled street. He delved deep into his pocket and produced two half-crowns which he thrust into her tiny hand. He closed her fingers so tightly on the coins that they cut into her soft fingers. That action was meant to install into her mind the need to watch them carefully. His conscience was clear and his duty to his god was complete. And so, my little great-grandmother Mary was banished from the shores of the only land she knew - the land that she would never stop dreaming of but the land to where she knew she could never return for she was guilty of 'The Sin of Eve.'

Mary had a son whom she christened Patrick Joseph. Patrick Joseph was brought up in the Gorbals and that blemish was added to that other blemish, he bore through no fault of his own – being a bastard! These blemishes would cost him his family and perhaps, his life when he crossed the path of Matilda Kerr!
I visited the Gorbals in the early sixties just to get an idea of the conditions young Patrick Joseph faced. Slum buildings there were in the process of being pulled down but the towering gables, soot-caked chimneys, treacherous stair-wells, smashed windows and rubble of ancient tenements blackly silhouetted against the night sky together with the bawling of drunks, stagger-

ing uncertainly in the rough direction of home, made me mutter: "If God is to be found here he is probably hiding behind some broken bill-board ; just like me."

With the 'Flight of the Irish Earls' to the continent in 1607 King James 1st of England (and 6th of Scotland) took the opportunity to take closer control of the province through the plantation of mainly lowland Scots and English from the border regions. His other reason was 'revenue'; it was easier to collect rents from the immigrants than it was to collect them from the natives. Two prominent families who owned swathes of land in the Ards Peninsula were the Gilmores and Kerrs; the former being Irish and the latter being of Scottish descent. The Gilmores either lost their lands through refusing to pay the rent or not being able to afford the cost. Kerrs lost their possessions through 'going native' or, to be more exact changing their religion from Presbyterian to Catholic. The change in circumstances did not alter their egotistic view that: 'they were families of note.' Matchmaking was rife in the nineteenth century and carried on well into the twentieth century so it is fair to assume Francis Gilmore and Matilda Kerr came together in that way. No matchmaker, worth his salt, would have attempted to unite two people who considered themselves to be from different stations in life, so a second assumption must be that the couple considered themselves to be equal. After they got married in 1875 equality ceased – Matilda, who was the elder by six years, became dominant. She and Francis have the dubious distinction of being my grand-parents but Matilda left no stone unturned in trying to prevent such an outcome.

Their married life began in the Gilmore family home which was the first house in Cloughey, or the last one, according to which end of the village one entered. It had a stable with outhouses attached and was considered to be quite upmarket in those days but little more than a hovel, by the time I took my first steps within its walls. The walls, of that old homestead, were up to three feet thick in places and must have been constructed from stones collected from the beach; for they were all shapes and sizes. By the time of our youth, the plaster and mortar were crumbling away and my younger brother had a habit of picking away at it and watching the sand trickle from the little holes he made.

"Mammy! Mammy! Mammy!" I ran into the house squealing: "Our James is dead!"

"Jamity-God-Almighty!" Mother charged out almost taking the half-door of its hinges: "Where is he?"

"He's lying under Tim's house," I stuttered.

"Under Tim's house? Jamity Christ! Jesus, Mary and Saint Joseph!"

We reached that little outhouse: now half a little outhouse; for the youngster was in the middle of a pile of stones – part of the wall had collapsed. Blood was seeping from his head and spurting with each beat of his little heart but he was conscious for, he was crying.

"You told me he was dead, you stupid get!" she ranted, picking the toddler up and rushing back into the house with him. "Go and tell Mister Keene to ring Doctor Duff – Immediately! Tell him to get Duff immediately!"

By the time I returned, my little brother had stopped crying and had a bandage on his head of such a size that any Sheik would have given a lot of rupees for it.

"There you are now: there you are, all bandaged up like an Egyptian mummy," Mother comforted him.

"Will he be able to thump people now he's a mammy," the other brother asked.

"I'll do the bloody thumping if you don't get out of here," she warned.

My predecessors, the Gilmores, had to pay ground rent to their landlords the Savages of Portaferry, who handed a percentage of that income over to Lord Dunleath of Ballywalter, who, in turn, gave another portion to the overall bosses; Lord Londonderry who was seldom in the country, much preferring London's society. It is comforting to know that the money went to a good cause rather than being wasted on starving victims of the potato famine. The Savages became 'Nugent' for obvious reasons but even with the new status they must have fallen on hard times for they offered my grandmother, Eliza Anne, the freehold of her own home for ten quid around about 1930.
She wrote back refusing the offer and stating: "The land was not yours in the first place! Who do you think you are; trying to sell me my own property?"

Eliza Anne Gilmore is the second tragic figure of my story. She was born in 1876 to Francis and Matilda Gilmore. From that date until 1934, she was firmly under the thumb of her mother, the grand matriarch; Matilda who was a big woman in more ways than stature and was totally indomitable. Her size, her attitude, her belief in her rightful status and the fact that she could read and write both in Irish and in English made her one tough old lady to deal with. In the mid eighteen hundreds few people could write in either language never mind both languages. Eliza Anne's brother: Francis was born in 1879 and went to sea when he was little more than a boy. On one sojourn, he brought home with him his friend; a small but very handsome man called Patrick Joseph Devaney. In the Gilmore household, Patrick Joseph was tolerated but not liked and all because of where he hailed from – the Gorbals! Although Eliza Anne, at six feet tall, towered over Patrick Joseph, she developed a crush on him. This was openly discouraged by the matriarch. Young Francis, the apple of his mother's eye, persisted in bringing his friend back to the old homestead and with each visit; Eliza Anne's love for Patrick Joseph grew and grew.

The old homestead was at the junction of two major parishes and was a meeting place for travelling bards, rag and bone men and gossipers of all shapes and sizes and also a safe-house for people of the Irish Republican Brotherhood. The most famous 'guest' of that particular organization would have been Maud Gonne's brother - John.

Maud Gonne was the long-time lover of the Irish writer, W B Yates. It was rumoured that Thomas Russell, 'The Man from God Knows Where,' whom the British executed in Downpatrick in 1803, also took refuge there, but I have not been able to confirm that. The gypsies would not have been made welcome there but would have been more so than Patrick Joseph Devaney when Matilda found out that he was illegitimate. Eliza Anne beseeched her mother to allow her to marry the good-looking young man from the Gorbals but the stern-faced Matilda refused uncompromisingly.

Francis Gilmore (junior) contacted, what was referred to, in those days as 'the tropical disease' but now thought to be malaria and died on Good Friday 1901. He was only twenty-two years of age. On his death-bed, he asked his mother to permit his sister: Eliza Anne, to marry Patrick Joseph. I am told that she just nodded her head as her tears flowed for the son she adored. No one had seen Matilda Kerr (now Gilmore) shed a single tear before that.

Although my paternal grandmother, Eliza Anne Devaney gave birth to two sons (Francis Anthony in 1904 and Patrick Joseph in 1906) Patrick

Joseph Senior was treated like dirt by my great-grandmother – Matilda. Frank, as he was later referred to, was said to be the 'smartest child that ever crossed the threshold of the Sand School.' Patrick Junior became my father and one of the very few people on this earth that I have allowed to influence me. Had I been able to choose a man to be my father that is the person I would have chosen.

This was the man who would lift me (as a child) into his arms, point up to the moon and ask:

"What size do you think that moon up there is?"

"About the size of a haystack," I guessed.

"Why do you say a haystack and not a farthing or even the size of Ireland?"

"'cause the Man on the Moon has got to sit on it, hasn't he?"

One day the shy, little man from the Gorbals left his wife and two small sons, Belfast bound to rejoin his ship in Glasgow. He never returned. The year was in 1916 and Patrick Joseph went out to sea on a convoy and Eliza Anne never saw or heard from him again. My grandmother convinced herself that his ship had been sunk but she never was officially informed of that and there was no way of tracing his listing as he had been sailing under an assumed name (catholics could not expect employment with Glasgow or Belfast shipping companies) his distraught wife did not know what that name was but I have a feeling it was 'John Brown'. Maybe, deep within, she suspected he deserted her and the children and it suited her better not to strive too hard for details. The two boys often stood on the beach and gazed out to sea, little hearts beating fast in hope as great sailing ships and old tramp steamers appeared in the offing beyond Cloughey Bay. This sad affair prompted me to write the poem; 'Skinny Wee Legs' (which I now append :)

Skinny Wee Legs

There he stood from the break of day
When the sun went down he went away
Asking sailors had they seen
'A boat that's called the Sovereign Queen.'
Wee red eyes scanned the sea
Skinny wee legs on a Belfast quay.
There he stood for months on end
Staring in the eyes of young seamen
Asking each one had he seen
'A man called Daddy from the Sovereign Queen.'
Wee red eyes scanned the sea
Skinny wee legs on a Belfast quay.
Then a sailor when he heard
Told the wee boy what he feared

'I'll never know where your father's been
But there is no ship called the Sovereign Queen'
Wee red eyes scanned the sea
Skinny wee legs on a Belfast quay.

Ninety per-cent of my father's life was spent at sea and in my police days he often came to my digs and listened to my exploits. It was from him that I probably got my sense of humour; Mother was more into slapstick. 'Pop' as I called him in those days used to pull at his eyebrows when he found something to be particularly amusing and he didn't fail to do so on hearing this tale:
As raw, police recruits we had to go through an exercise called 'Fire Rescue'. It involves identifying a number written on a stone in a room filled with smoke. A smoke-bomb was placed in a certain corner and a stone in the adjacent corner. If you crawled in with your nose to the floor, the stone was simple enough to find as the smoke was lighter than air. I tucked myself into the queue just ahead of a couple of reluctant fatties. By this time the word had got out as to where the stone could be found. I crawled in, found the stone, held my breath, got to my feet and put it on a window-sill. As a bonus I moved the smoke-bomb nearer the door so that the draught caught it swirling the smoke about more than it

was supposed to do. The first fatty in spluttered and coughed so much the instructor had to call him out. The next one had to be rescued. For that little prank, I got a couple of week's jankers.

I got a further week for my next venture. On entering the swimming baths I noticed a strange piece of wood that closely resembled a turd. I picked it up, hid it in my swimming trunks and jumped into the pool. A little lady, P C Monk was my life-saving partner. As she rescued me in one of the exercises, I complained that I had an immediate urge to 'go!'

"Can you not hold on until this rescue is over?"

"Afraid not!"

I swam over to the steps, pulled down my trunks and released the dirty old bit of branch. It floated to the top immediately and PC Monk beat such a hasty retreat she could have qualified for the Olympics. Soon the word spread and panic set in; some hauling themselves out of the pool whilst other dived under the 'floater' and headed for the steps.

"Devaney! Get out of the pool and get your clothes on," it was the instructor, Acting Sergeant Knipe, "And Devaney! Take that piece if shit with you!"

"But Foulds is innocent, Sergeant!" (Foulds was one of the fatties).
"Not Foulds – that crap, or whatever it is!"
As I made my way along the changing booths, I heard a whimper from one of them. I looked under the door and saw that it was occupied. One of the recruits was in there shaking like a leaf; he was terrified of water. That was his last day in the Lancashire Constabulary but needless-to-say, any time ale was consumed, I and my special floater got the blame.
The following morning as we left the commandant's disciplinary hearing Knipe whispered in my ear: "The commandant is determined to show you that it is harder to get out of this force than to stay in it."
He, for one, caught on to my cunning plan to get an early ship back to Ireland.

It wasn't long after that, that I had another run-in with Knipe. One day, in the gymnasium, I spied three or four fatties lifting weights. I looked at the weight they were lifting and reckoned it couldn't be much more than seventy or eighty pounds. The biggest fatty added a couple of pounds more, lifted it above his head through the classic 'clean and jerk' then raised his arms in the air and awaited acclaim.

I walked over to him, “Wee girls could lift that.”
“Oh aye, Paddy? Let’s see you do it then!”
“One hand or two?” I asked.
“Come on then, just fucking lift it!”
I lifted it with one hand. I was confident I could for both my parents were exceptionally strong and I knew what weight I could lift. It was simply a matter of genes. But as I held the bar above my head, I felt it get lighter.
“Should have added a few more pounds," was my first reaction.
“I have taken the strain; you simply let go and walk away,” it was Acting Sergeant Knipe and I could tell that he was in a foul mood.
“If you ever do that again I will have you fined a month’s wages. What were you thinking of man?”
“Eh … eh … the clean and jerk, Sergeant, them ones there are alright at the jerking but that’s about it”
“You were just showing off to the police women. If you must do such silly things, then use the short bar which is the proper equipment for single-hand lifting, and Devaney!”
“Yes Sergeant?”
“You would need to lift twice that amount to beat Precious McKenzie and he’s half your size.”
“Yes Sergeant?”

"Devaney, you just remember this: no matter how good you are at anything, there is someone out there who is better."
"Yes Sergeant?"

Back to the Gilmore Clan struggle: I'm told Matilda's pride took a hammering for her and her daughter, Eliza Anne, had to earn a crust by whatever means they could and that included repairing clothes, making sheets out of flour sacks and selling cups of tea to any traveller who could afford it. Collecting driftwood for a winter fire would have been commonplace and any other 'bits and pieces', they perchance came by could have been sold on to the rag-and-bone man, who incidentally, was still 'on the go' in my young days. The minute the two lads looked like becoming men they were packed off to find steady work; Frank labouring on building sites with his younger brother Patrick helping out on an old lorry transporting stones, gravel and occasionally mortar.

Some years later Frank joined the newly formed Free State Army whilst Patrick found work as a deck boy on a rusty old coaster and had to take his 'donkey's breakfast' with him, under his arm. A 'donkey's breakfast' was a slang term for a canvass bag filled with straw that sailors put under their heads when having a sleep. When a seaman became better established he got a hammock which was slung in positions according to the 'below decks pecking order.' By the twenties, steamships had almost edged out sailing ships but my father would have seen the majestic barques like the 'Herzogen Cecilie', the 'Pomeranian' and the 'Parma' go sailing by with their heavily canvassed arms reaching high into the clouds. These 'windjammers' as sailors referred to them, still carried bulk cargoes such as rice, coal, saltpetre and especially guano, deep-sea via Cape Horn and the Cape of Good Hope having retained much of their former share of that type of market. A boy sailor hadn't much of a life for when he was not scrubbing decks, painting anything that didn't move or fending off homosexuals he was below decks splicing ropes and practising the endless types of mariner's knots. Any spare time he did get he would be expected to entertain the older hands by bare-fist boxing his young contemporaries for a few coppers that just might be thrown into the ring if the old sea-dogs were sufficiently impressed or pissed—as the case may be.

We can never pass a final judgment that old Patrick Joseph lies at the bottom of the deep-blue sea until we consider two strange happenings:
In 1965 I was resident in Chorley where I met an old man called Ted Bolan. I had a drink with him and he asked my name and from what part of Ireland I came. When I informed him he told me he once sailed with a man; "a long, long time ago," called "Devaney" from down "that part of the country – a man called 'Patrick Devaney.'"
I said, "Oh, that would be my father – he is called Patrick"
Old Ted told me the name of the ship but I can't remember it now.
My father knew the ship but told me that he had never sailed in it: "maybe it was your auld grandfather, my own father," he remarked
My father did not remember a Ted Bolan. The latter would have been over eighty years of age when I met him, putting him more in the generation of old Patrick than his son but at that age perhaps his memory did not serve him well.

It was at that time that 'Pop' told me a strange tale:
In the late thirties when my father himself had been at sea for some time; he was coming off a

ship in Liverpool docks when he saw a little old man staring at him intensely:
"Oh my god that looks like my da'," he gasped and then simply walked past him. A bit further on he turned and looked back – the little old man was looking back too. But my father went on his way for he too was a shy man – like father: like son - but I could tell, when he told the story, he regretted the decision he made that day in Liverpool.

A long time before that, in the parish of Carrickmannon, ten miles away, as the crow flies, if the crow is prepared to fly across Strangford Lough there lived a young man, who, although he didn't know it at the time, was to become my maternal grandfather. His name was James McCartan, and to say the least; he was different. Perhaps it was his terrible accident that caused 'Granda' to lack somewhat in social decorum. If someone arrived just as the dinner was being served - it was James McCartan. If someone was first on the dance floor – it was James McCartan. If someone stood up to make an uninvited speech at a wedding – it was James McCartan. People referred to him as: 'The man himself.' I suppose that's as nice a way of putting as one could expect!

When James McCartan was a young man he worked on a farm. One day, during the harvesting season, he went missing. Eventually, someone noticed a large haystack had fallen over. In those days farm hands prided in building corn and hay stacks as high as two-story houses and sometime a lot bigger. Just on chance, the workers began clearing the tumbled stack, and there he was, lying there - apparently lifeless. No amount of throwing water on him could revive the young man and so he was carted off to the hospital. My grandfather never fully recovered from that tragedy, suffering thereafter from epileptic fits and relentless nightmares to such a degree that we cannot possible imagine. He spent a big part of his life in a mental institution and even after he was declared sane enough to be released, the lady, who was to be my grandmother - Mary Elisabeth Brown (by that time McCartan) – refused to sign him out and indicated that she did not want him back until she was beyond childbearing age. James McCartan's mother together with his brother, Terence, eventually signed him out and he went back home to live with his wife. His brothers pleaded with my grandfather never to return to Mary Elizabeth, because of what she had done, but they eventually reconciled themselves to the fact that he still loved and wanted be be with that particular woman.

Mary Elisabeth Brown was from a staunch family of nationalist supporters from south Down and the whole family were fluent in the Gallic language as is typical of descendents of those who change allegiance. After the demise of her husband, my maternal grandmother, had a tough life indeed for then it was she who had to go out and 'earn a crust' to feed her family of three. She was a proud woman. She was, above all else, an Irish woman and it was beneath her dignity to have to slave for a direct descendent of an English landlord.

The first child born to Mary McCartan was a hefty daughter christened her Margaret Teresa, and that lady later became my mother. Her mother, due to the circumstances she found herself in, had to rule her family with a 'rod of iron' but Margaret Theresa took that to be the norm and carried it into the lives of her offspring. In my police years, I marvelled at my colleague's devotion to their mothers; some even having 'MUM' tattooed on their knuckles. I could not possibly imagine being so close to my mother as that. It was like an undeclared war between the pair of us with me losing more battles than the Irish and Italians lumped together. Margaret Theresa did not receive the nickname 'The Targe' for nothing for some of the punishments I received from her was little short of brutality:

- Beaten with a floor-brush until the head flew off it.
- Beaten with a mop until the shaft broke over my back.
- Punched instead of being slapped as other parents would have done.
- Had a poker, which had been aimed at my back, lodge in the scullery door.
- Had a similar experience but this time the weapon of choice was a gully-knife.
- Beaten over the head with an aluminium saucepan until I almost lost consciousness.
- Had teacups, saucers and plates aimed at me only to smash into the walls.

My mother suffered from having a vile temper and, in this day and age, she would have been locked up for cruelty. None of her children confided in her, for her first reaction was always a violent attack. One day my baby brother dashed towards the gate as a bus was passing. I jammed a bit of wood I was using as a hurley-stick across the gate. He crashed into it, splitting open his little mouth but he did not go under the wheels of the bus. Of course, my little brother told the Targe that I hit him with the stick. No explanation was permitted; I was beaten for ten to fifteen minutes, which was a normal occurrence. But I have to admit, some punishments were not totally unwarranted; I defied her throughout my young days. I don't think I accepted her as my mother and certainly did not see her as my superior and this might all be down to re-incarnation. For example, when she shouted at me that I was nothing but 'a lousy bastard' I would reply: "You can hardly blame me for that."

In that age of cruelty, violence was not confined to the home; schoolchildren were disciplined through the use of it. I am quite sure sadism was involved for there was one particularly relief teacher who caned us severely because our bus was late arriving due to heavy snow. Punishment was meted out to me as one of the brighter children but for the less fortunate souls, punishment could range from punching with clenched fists to being lifted up by the ears and dropped on the floor. It is little wonder parents arrived at school and often took frightful revenge; unfortunately, that would be the last day in the education of the relevant child. He or she would be completely ignored from then onwards. No jotter, no pencil, not any pen and ink bottle would be handed out to the youngster; he or she would have effectively become ostracized. I never once admitted to my mother that I had been treated cruelly and not simply because of the fear of becoming a 'persona non grata', but because she would most likely have dished out an additional form of punishment that would have gone off the 'Richter Scale.'

It would not be fair to lump all teachers together under the banner titled: "Cruelty." One teacher I know of turned aside and shed a tear when he looked down at a child's feet. The boy had walked to school through slush and snow in a pair of plimsolls that had little or no soles left in them. The newspaper that lined the footwear was soaking wet and oozing out of the sides. That kind teacher bought that little boy a pair of leather shoes, which were mended, time after time, and handed down to several other members of the family.

Mother never tired of reminding us that she had to walk to school in heavy, wooden clogs in the winter time and in her bare feet in the summer time and it was the latter that caused her to lose one of her little toes:

"What happened to your wee toe," I enquired
"A big, heavy iron drain cover sliced it off "
"Did you fall down the drain?"
"No! I lost a couple of marbles down the drain and the buggers that were supposed to be holding it up let it drop."
"Did you tell Missus Magee about it?"
"Can't remember, why?"
"She told Sadie O'Rourke, she thought you had lost your marbles."
"Oh she did, did she? She will hear about that!"

As a teenager, my future mother's first love encounter did not go down well with my grandmother; Margaret Theresa fell for a protestant. Swift and decisive action was called for and it came in the form of Arthur McCartan the youngest brother of her father; Jim McCartan. According to reports, Arthur was a good-looking man himself and no young girl in her right mind would refuse a pillion seat on a motorbike, probably the only such vehicle in the district. Whether Arthur fancied himself as a match-maker or not I never found out but that is certainly the role he volunteered for in that momentous 'tour of eligible bachelors'. Margaret rejected all that was presented to her. When she said, 'NO!' she meant NO! And on and on it went until the day

Arthur took her to see Eliza Anne Devaney from beside the Sand School in the parish of Ballygalget, in the lower Ards Peninsula.

There Margaret Theresa was presented to a man, some four inches taller than Arthur and with the good looks of his father; Patrick Joseph Devaney, the little man who was said to have been lost at sea during the first world war. Margaret Teresa said, 'Yes' and at last I (and six others) became a probability. The matriarch, Matilda, had died some five years earlier (1932) and so the way was clear for my paternal grandmother was a much milder mannered lady than my great-grandmother. Margaret Theresa simply could not have lived with Matilda – they were too alike. It wasn't long before Patrick and Margaret settled into the house that we, young ones called: 'The Old Homestead.'

If only at that time, Margaret Theresa McCartan had known that one day, she would be out searching for her three little boys not realizing they were ten feet underneath where she stood, she might have had second thoughts on becoming Margaret Theresa Devaney:
On Cloughey beach, there is a concrete and cast-iron structure we called 'The burn.' The burn is

really the trickle of water that flows through that structure. Well, it flowed through it until some pilot tried to land his aeroplane on the shore and crashed into it cutting it in half; so, until this very day the rivulet flows out of the side of the concrete and iron structure. The culvert that takes the water underneath the main road, through Cloughey village, is a cast-iron pipe, a couple of feet in diameter. It was up that cast-iron pipe that we, three small lads, set out on an adventure that could have had catastrophic results.

Teke was sent up in front, just in case I had to face one of the very large eels that used the stream to reach their breeding ground. I, Gomez, went in second and little Jap brought up the rear.
"What happens if we get stuck up here behind a big stone or something?" Teke asked me.
"Jap can crawl back and get Mister Keene to dig us out."
"Mister Keene can't dig; he only sells sweets."
"Get Pat McKeating then!"
"He'd better get Tammy Dougherty; he has got a long shovel."
"It wouldn't reach up this far," little Jap intervened.
"Shut up; we're not going to get stuck!" I shouted.

We bloody well were!
Teke, up front decided to let a fart. Gomez, with his nose to close to Teke's ass, couldn't stick the smell in the confined space so decided to turn around.

There was I, neck and shoulders wedged up against one side of the rusty old pipe and my ass wedged up against the other side.
"I'm stuck!"
"What we going to do," asked Teke, who, being smaller than I, had managed to turn around.
"I'll go back and get Mammy," Jap suggested.
"No! No! Don't get her, get Mister Keene."
"But you said he hadn't got any shovel"
"I didn't say he had no shovel, just get him."
Off he went.
It was then that I had an idea and instructed my other brother: "You lie down and kick me 'round with your feet."
"If I lie down I'll get drowned."
"Just get lying down; hold unto the sides of the pipe and push on my bum with your feet."
It worked and we emerged and quickly scurried off to hide amongst the sand dunes for we knew Mister Keene would be appearing soon.

"Hello, up there, can anyone hear me?" shouted Mister Keene, in his post London accent.
"Maybe the eels have got them," suggested young Jap.
"That is highly unlikely! Hello, up there!" Mister Keene got down on one knee, "you go and get your mother, whilst I phone for the fire-brigade."
"No don't do that!" I stopped laughing and jumped up from my hiding place.
Mister Keene was not the most pleasant person in our village and, at that moment, he was even less pleasant for he shouted: "If you children think I have nothing to do other than be the subject of your silly pranks, then I shall have to have words with your mother."
"It wasn't a plank …" Jap stuttered
"Goodbye!" Mister Keene stormed off, luckily for us, towards his shop and not our house.

Both my mother and father encouraged us to be competitive if not good sportsmen (in the sense of being fair) and this competitiveness was still with me when I was training to be a policeman. The biggest mistake I made was volunteering to play hockey – not knowing the first thing about the game. I suppose it wasn't quite like that:

My friend Knipe stuck his head around the door and shouted: "We're a man short; anyone here play hockey?"

"I played hurley," I responded foolishly.

"You'll do."

The first ball that came in my direction was still in the air when I connected with it and almost wrecked that little wooden stopper they have at the back of the net.

'Whistle – foul!'

"Why?"

"You are supposed to stop the ball before you hit it"

"What's the point in that?"

"That's the rules."

A defender stopped the ball in front of his own goal:

"This is a good opportunity," thought I, and took a swipe at it, landing, not only the ball, but the defender's hockey stick as well, in the back of the net.

'Whistle – foul!'

"Why?"

"You are not supposed to bulldoze your opponent's stick off him"

"You can in hurley."

"This is not hurley."

Again, a defender had the ball just in front of his own goal but one of my team-mates was fiddling around trying to dispossess him.

"Another good opportunity," thought I, landing feet first in the melee and swiping about in all directions.

'Whistle – foul!'

"Why?"

"Never mind why – you are off – take an early bath and I'll have a word with Sergeant Knipe, about his selection methods, after the game."

My brother, Patrick was probably the most competitive of the whole family; playing third division football in England, being a weight-lifting champion in the prison service and no mean badminton player on top of that. However, his greatest achievement must have been as 'Teke' on a little bicycle with neither gears nor brakes on it:

We heard about the big bicycle race – the 'Milk Race,' for professional cyclist's only, was to pass through our little village. So, on a sunny Saturday afternoon, he patiently sat on his little contraption, behind the myrtle bushes, awaiting the arrival of the leading contenders. Suddenly, tension showed in his face as he spied the race leader make his way from Magean's Corner and

along the main road towards where he was hidden. Even at that distance of half-a-mile we could see that the professional was kitted out in bright, flash colours. However, that did not deter Teke; he had no intention of simply joining the peloton as a 'nobody'' it was the lead he was after and nothing short of it. He launched his little, old 'sit up and beg' from its camouflage and went off in hasty pursuit.
Our butcher, Jamsie McDowell, summed it up best when talking to my mother: "Oh Jesus God, Missus, we're all sitting on the shore-wall dyke when here's this cyclist body in a big fancy racing bike, flying up the road and there, right behind him, was this wee fellow, in a rusty old bike and his wee feet were turning them pedals so bloody fast there was sparks coming out of the chain."

In Teke' time away: all we could do was sit and wait. It must have been over an hour later when he returned. He emerged from a different direction than from where his little ass had disappeared on his chase of the professional. He came from down the Quarter Brea which meant he had been to Portaferry and back out along the lough, to a place called Granshaw – a distance of twelve miles.

"Did you beat him?" enquired Jap.
"Na, he didn't want me with him no more!"
"How did you know," I asked
"He turned round and said, "Why don't you just fuck off son?"

But back to my dubious volunteering to take part in sporting competitions during my police trainee days: it appeared; I had volunteered for the rugby team – me – all ten and a half stones – very likely indeed! Never-the-less: the team sheet was posted and there was no mistaking the name or number; PC 2075 Devaney:
"Bloody Knipe!" I swore
Anyhow, the game started and I was doing fine until someone decided to pass me the ball. I flew up the wing but there blocking my way was something, just a feature and a few pounds short of being classified as a gorilla. The next thing I remember is both the ball and I were in touch and I felt as if I had been run over by Fred Dibnah's traction engine.
I spent the rest of the match shouting: "I don't want that fucking ball!"
"Why," asked the captain
"Look! Just give it to that gorilla over there; he seems to need it more than I do."

One day we filed into the gymnasium and a lot of faces dropped for there on the table lay a couple of dozen pairs of boxing gloves.

"I hope he pairs me with one of the fatties," I mentioned to my big buddy, Dave Crosby.

"I'm a big fatty and I'm not putting the gloves on against no Irishman, no Scotsman and nobody from Liverpool for that matter," Dave asserted.

"You're not a big fatty; you're just well built – if perhaps, a little timid."

"Right!" Knipe hollered; "has anybody here done any boxing before?"

I had done a little bit, in a club in Belfast during my teens, but I wasn't daft enough to volunteer that information. A curly, ginger-haired lad, who turned out to be homosexual, raised his hand.

"Anyone else: Devaney?"

"Oh here we go again!" I muttered.

"No, Sergeant, a bit of street fighting, but that hardly counts," I laughed

"That'll do, pick a pair of gloves that fit. You, Ginger and I are going to teach this mob how to take care of themselves."

There were twenty-six in the class, so we got eight each. Included in my batch were two fat-ties – one of whom was my mate Dave Crosby. The change in a man's eyes will tell you when he is about to deliver a punch so it wasn't too difficult to avoid being hit or just to catch the punch on a glove from pure beginners. I was really tempted to give the other fatty a dig in the solar-plexus, but he was so pathetic I felt sorry for him. He wasn't the worst though; there was a very tall and skinny lad that simply hadn't a clue.

Knipe caught me nipping around behind that lad and demanded: "Devaney what in the name of God are you doing?"

"He keeps closing his eyes! He doesn't know where I am, Sergeant."

"OK, put him on the punch-bag."

"I'd have my money on the punch-bag!"

"Just carry on with the others; who knows, there just might be a Joe Louis amongst them - though none of them even look the right colour from where I'm standing?"

When it came Dave's turn, I gave him a tap on the stomach and he went down like a ton of bricks.

"Get up, Dave!"

"No I won't: it's safer down here. Are you not supposed to count me out or something?"

"You didn't even get punched properly."

"If Jack Johnston can get away with it, so can I," Crosby groaned to emphasize the point.

When I was in my twenties, I was timed over one hundred yards at 10.3 seconds, which is extremely fast in the Ards Peninsula but extremely slow against Olympians, not to mention the steroid guzzlers. When I ran out of human opposition I used to practice by chasing cats; dogs were no good as they had a habit of waiting on you. As the fastest policeman in the section, I was called on one day to catch a criminal whose method of avoiding detention was to out-sprint his would-be captors. His favourite hiding place was on terrain impassable by car or motorbike. I was brought in and they flushed him out. He had about ten yards start on me but after a hundred yards, or so, I could almost lay a hand on him but that is where it ended; after another fifty yards I was five yards behind him and losing ground. The truth was: he was not only fast but he was a stayer as well – a most unusual thing indeed. Eventually, it took a police dog to catch him; one that didn't wait on anyone.

It was the lack of staying power that got me into trouble in the compulsory cross-country runs at the police college. I always finished second last and my mate Dave finished last as I used to humiliate him on the home straight by out-sprinting him. Acting Sergeant Knipe, the PTI, eventually got fed up seeing us finish behind the fatties and even those with sick-notes, so he set us the task of finishing in the top fifteen or facing jankers. However, we had a cunning plan. A mile or so from the start we deviated through the policewomen's billets and spent a considerable length of time lying in the sunshine; smoking. Unfortunately, we had not noted the time we started out and therefore, had no indication as to when to rejoin the other runners on the finishing straight. After, what seemed a long time; we began peeping over the wall to see if there was any sign of the leaders.

After another while Dave Crosby said: "What if they are all in by now?"

"Yea, it seems like ages. We'll be in bigger trouble if we are slower than usual."

"I agree, they must have all passed by; let's head off," Dave suggested.

There did not appear to be anything unusual as we approached the finishing line as competitors had the habit of running on through - straight to the showers where they had left their kit.

Knipe blew a loud blast for me, as I again, outsprinted big Dave in the last one hundred yards,

"Well done, Devaney! Bravo, Crosby, you both have just broken the course record by over five minutes, with no sign of even breaking into a sweat. I do not know how you did it but I look forward to meeting you at the commandant's disciplinary parade tomorrow morning."

With my attitude, of not giving a damn as to whether I was kicked out or not, I was prepared to suffer a lot less regimental styled bullshit than the others and one particularly incident comes to mind, which involved a drill sergeant called Halpin:

If anything went wrong on parade, irrespective of who caused it, Sergeant Halpin would holler, in a screechy voice: "Devaney!"

On one particular drill session, involving a completely different class he yelled out: "Devaney – get back in line, boy!"

One day, he had us all double marching with greatcoats on and my mate Dave told me he just couldn't take any more.

So, in an imitation of Halpin's squeaky voice I yelled out: "At the double, on the spot, quick march!"

It worked; the whole intake ground to a halt and then began marching on the spot.

Out came Sergeant Halpin's pocket-book in a flash: "Devaney! Commandant's disciplinary parade; seven-thirty am, sharp!"

A bit of camp 'bullshit' was to march offenders, 'at the double' into the commandant's office where they were further required to cut him off a smart salute.

"You are charged with the very serious offence of insubordination through countermanding Sergeant Halpin's command whilst on the parade ground, what have you to say in answer to the charge?" the commandant asked.

"I hereby counter-charge Sergeant Halpin with discrimination – which is an even more serious charge!" I replied.

"What is the evidence for such a charge?" the senior officer asked.

"He just guessed it was me, as he does when anything goes wrong while we are drilling! The voice, Sir, sounded so shrill and squeaky it must have come from a Welshman."

The Chief Superintendent, ignored my frivolity and turned to Halpin: "Sergeant?"

"I am absolutely sure it was Devaney, Sir."

"Are you accusing me of being a Welshman," I interrupted.

Halpin did not reply.

That gave me the opportunity to go on the attack;

"If you would permit, Sir, I would ask Sergeant Halpin to name just one other person on my intake!"

"Well Sergeant?" The commandant nodded in his direction.
"Well there's … there's … there's Devaney … Devaney, of course … and eh … and …"
"And!" the chief officer became impatient.
After what must have been an embarrassing silence – for both men, the Chief turned to me" Well, that will be all, for the moment, PC Devaney … Sergeant, you remain behind."
I heard no more on the charges but from that day onward Sergeant Halpin completely ignored me.

Quite a few from that intake went on to be high-ranking officers. One, in particular, years later, came on the television during a news bulletin.
I shouted at my wife: "Look, look! See that chief superintendent there? He trained with me. His father was a chief superintendent too."
"And he learned his lessons better than you, by the looks of things," she responded.
I didn't tell her that that same person, as a lanky, gawky, floppy-eared, long-toothed recruit 'broke his duck' in the field of passion as a result of big Dave and I paying a grubby, old hag a small gin and five Woodbine. I remember telling him that he would be obliged to marry her under the circumstances of her being with child.

"That's not likely to happen though, is it?" he asked.
Nobody could answer him for laughing. Incidentally, that happened in a place called the 'Blackpool Plough' and the next time we visited, that establishment of ill-repute, the same, old hag recognized us and had the cheek to ask: "Hello! Any one here fancy the same deal as last time?"
A newcomer turned to Dave and me: "Don't tell me you … well bloody hell … wait until I get back to the billets!"

As the passing-out parade day approached nervous tension built amongst the recruits and most of it was down to prospective postings.
"If you have not behaved yourself you can expect one of the rough dives such as Kirby, Widnes or Huyton. Devaney's a cert for one of them," some wise-gut cracked.
"I couldn't give a fiddler's fuck!" I replied.
However, I found my fingers crossed as I stood in front of Assistant Chief Constable Lineker:
"Kirby, Widnes, Huyton … Kirby, Widnes, Huyton. …" I repeated to myself.
After Lineker scanned through my report to remind himself of whom he was going to talk to, he shook his little grey head: "Now this report I do not like! On reading it, I asked myself:

‘Would this man not be better off joining the opposition?’”

“The opposition, Sir – sorry!”

“The criminal fraternity! I have dealt with many from that walk of life, as you may well imagine, Devaney, in the many years I have been a policeman, and they are quite a number. I have known people who have served time for lesser offences than those I see, set out, before me.”

“Kirby, Widnes, Huyton … Kirby, Widnes, Huyton . … or the next boat home,” I contemplated.

“The only saving grace is contained in the last line of this report. Do you know what it says Devaney?” Lineker continued, after I had concluded that it was all over.

“Eh … eh … Kirby, eh, Widnes … I mean no, Sir! I haven't a clue!”

“’Will make a good police officer’ – that’s what your instructor says! How he comes to that conclusion from this report I simply do not understand!”

“Kirby, Widnes, Huyton … Kirby, Widnes, Huyton . …” I still had my fingers crossed.

“PC 2075 Devaney you are to be posted to Widnes,” the little assistant chief informed,

“Report first thing on Monday next; to the main police station of that town.

"Kirby, Widnes, Huyton ... Kirby, Widnes, Widnes! – that's one of them – bloody Widnes!"

"That will be all PC Devaney."

Incidentally, the lanky, gawky, floppy eared, long toothed, son of a chief superintendent got a cosy posting which, ironically, took in the Blackpool Plough. I would have given a lot just to have been with him when he attended those premises on duty for the first time.

In the police, I went on to face some potentially dangerous incidents but none quite as dangerous as my brother faced when he was little more than five or six years of age. We decided to build a sea-going raft. Its chance of gaining a sea-worthiness certificate was not great.

"Teke, you and Jap go and gather some wood and I'll build us a ship called 'The Bussler.'"

"Why has it to be called the Bussler, Gomez, could we not call it the Titanic?" the younger of my little brothers wanted to know.

"No we can't call it the Titanic, 'cause the Germans sunk it!"

"Why did they sink it?" asked the littlest one.

"'cause it was war and they sailed an iceberg into it."

"Why did Germans sail an iceberg into it?"

“’cause our daddy had sunk all their destroyers, and they had to use the icebergs,” I informed and no one there was in a position to question the historical accuracy of the statement. As a matter of fact, I believed the Second World War was a personal confrontation between my father and ‘Auld Hitler’. The morning the war came to a close; my mother lifted me above her head yelling excitingly: “The war is over! The war is over! Auld Hitler is dead!”

“Did Daddy kill him?” was all I asked.

“We could call it the Oriana,” my other brother suggested.

“Why do you want to call it the Oriana?”

“’cause you could row it if the sails get shot down.”

“Daddy says it’s thousands and thousands and thousands of tons, so you couldn’t row it and anyway, it has no sails.”

The ‘Good Ship Bussler’ was tied up to a rusty old ring on the burn structure to await shipping orders.

The three of us, brothers were joined by our little mates, Muddle and Flint for the official launching of the great vessel. It truly was a magnificent sight; bits of floorboard, hardboard and driftwood were secured together by binder twine and rusty nails of all sizes. Additional buoyancy was obtained by fastening a sealed tin to each corner. A bicycle saddle, ripped and exposing rusty old springs, was screwed down somewhere 'amidships' to provide the 'Captain' with a seat.

"You have to smash a bottle of stout on it to make it launch proper," Muddle informed.

"We haven't got a bottle of stout," Teke told him.

"We could use one of them bottles Missus Gillis throws out of her shop," Flint suggested.

"Go and get one then," I instructed.

Flint, Muddle and Jap scurried off and returned a few minutes later, with a full bottle of HP sauce, which looked about tens years beyond a safe selling date.

"I'll be 'the skipper'," I declared unilaterally, "Now who wants to be 'mate'?

"I want to be a skipper too;" Teke protested.

"Well you can't be a skipper for boats have only one skipper and I'm him; you can be the mate; that's a good job when you go to sea."

"I want to be a mate, too," Muddle requested

I shook my little fair head: "No, you have to the bosun."

"What does a bosun do?"

"He gives things out to the crew."

"Alright then, I'll be the bosun."
"What am I?" Jap requested a position on the important ship.
"You can be a deck-hand."
"What does a deck-hand do?"
"He decks people."
"What for?"
"For being late for duty."
"Alright, I'll be a deck-hand then."
"I want to be the anchor man," Flint told me.
"You can't be the anchor man, 'cause, we haven't got any anchor."
"What can I be then?"
"You can be the cook."
"I don't want to be the cook."
"Why?"
"'cause Captain Cook, got threw overboard when he ran out of sausages."
"Let him be the purser then," Teke suggested.
"Does he get the most money?"
"Yes, the skipper hands him a purse with all the wages in it and he has to hand it out to the crew," I was getting a bit fed-up.
"Alright, I'll be the purser then."

The Bussler was unceremoniously dragged unto the current of the burn to propel it on its way to the open sea. All that occurred was the gouging out of a couple of deep grooves in the sand, which quickly diverted rivulets of the precious floating fluid and the only thing that moved at all was one of our buoyancy tins that had come loose. It certainly did not augur well for the Irish shipbuilding industry. Eventually, after much pushing and dragging by the crew, the little craft reached the vastness of the Irish Sea.

"The skipper is first to go on board and every-one else has to ask permission to come on after him," I announced.

It didn't take long for a potential mutiny to threat-en for all the crewmen jumped aboard at the same time or thereabouts. The gallant little raft sank to the bottom of the sea – which was about eighteen inches down at that particular place.

"There is too many of the crew aboard! I an-nounced, "Some people will have to 'jump ship.'"

Nobody moved!

"There needs to be some land-lubbers," I told them.

There were no volunteers so the skipper stepped off to see if the Bussler came to the surface. It didn't.

"There needs to be some more get off to be dock-ers," I shouted.

Once again: nobody moved, so the captain reverted to sixteenth-century tactics – by throwing mutineers overboard.

When the Good Ship Bussler resurfaced, I announced: "Now let me board first and the rest of you can get on when I shout out your names."
I stepped aboard; it sank!
"You need to get some scuppers," Muddle suggested.
"Scuppers would have to suck up nearly all of the Irish Sea," I said, with a gloomy face," this ship is going to have to go to sea without its skipper."
"I'll get on; I'll try it; Teke shouted eagerly.
"You still have to ask the skipper for permission," I had to save face, somehow.
"Permission to get up?"
"That's not how you say it – 'Permission to get onboard, is what you say,'" I insisted
"Permission to get up on board, Skipper?"
"Permission granted – get up."
Luckily, or unluckily, as it turned out: the raft remained afloat. One by one, the other crew members tried to join the mate but each time the Bussler went down to the bottom.
"Maybe we should have called it 'The Titanic?' Flint moaned.

"Shut up and give that seaman his oars," I instructed.
"Them's called butter clappers," Jap informed me.
"They's called oars and you'd better not tell Mammy we took them."
"Where have I to row the boat to?" the first mate enquired.
"The Isle of Man," I replied
"Where's the Isle of Man?"
"That's it over there," I pointed to the blue shape on the distant horizon.
"How far is the Isle of Man?"
"Out past the Rig."

Great and mightily dangerous rocks surround Cloughey bay, from the South Rock to the North Rock and in between; the Ridge, Crooked Pladdy and the submerged but treacherous, Cannon Rock upon which many a ship broke her back. Over the years, ships from across the world met their end on that part of the Irish coast. Many were the mornings; we awoke to find a great ship high and dry on one of those immovable, sea monsters. The rock formation causes strong currents and eddies to form and it was into this death trap, we watched our little brother furiously paddle bits and pieces of wood bound together by the weak hands of small children.

Poor Teke was little more than a dot on the horizon when the Englishman, Mister Keene rushed down the embankment.

"Who is that out there? Is that a little boy out there?" he demanded an answer.

Frederick Keene had a very powerful brass telescope which he used constantly during the war to watch allied and axes shipping in the Irish Sea. Mother's good friend, Lilly Gibson, reckoned there was more to it and that, in fact, he was watching for the arrival of an old battle-axe of a wife he had abandoned in London.

"How would he know she was on board," my mother wanted to know.

"It's reported she built her own ship and rigged it up with a pair of knickers to outrun the best auld windjammers that ever sailed them there waters," Lilly replied.

Our little Bussler would not have matched up to the Lilly Gibson's fantasy barque but the difference was: our boat was real and it was a real boy that was paddling it towards the horizon as Mister Keene bounced up and down on the silver sands like someone going out of his mind.

"Where is that child heading? How much further will he go out?" Mister Keene stormed at us.
"Isle of Man," I replied rather nonchalantly.
"That young boy out there, it's your brother isn't it?" he screamed at me, waving his arms frantically.
The small dot on the horizon must have seen Mister Keene waving for he appeared to acknowledge him by waving back with his butter-clappers.
"What is he doing now? That's dangerous; he could slip into the sea, if he keeps doing that."
"That's called 'semaphore."
"Well, what's he saying; what's he doing?"
"He's coming back."
"Why, why is he not going to the Isle of Man?" Jap asked me.
"I think he's getting hungry," I shook my shoulders, as I couldn't be really certain of that.
"He forgot to take a fishing rod with him," Jap told Mister Keene.
"He had no frying-pan as well," Muddle added.

Frederick Keene paced up and down the beach, sometimes in the water and sometimes on the sand: "I must, I really must phone for the lifeboat, inform the coast-guards! This could be a tragedy!"

"He's nearly back past the Rig now," my eagle-eyed smaller brother informed us.

"How do you know; how can you be sure of that?" Mister Keene growled at him.

"His head's getting bigger."

I think it is fair to add here, that, that was indeed, the case, and it continued to get bigger for the rest of his days.

Fred Keene became calmer with every minute that passed as he seemed to accept, to a lesser degree than us, that Teke was truly an able-bodied seaman. Nevertheless, he waded into the sea until it was almost up to his neck as my brother approached the docking area.

"Ahoy there shipmate!" I greeted the seafarer as a dripping-wet; Mister Keene glanced at me in disgust.

"Did you see any sharks?" Muddle asked Teke.

"No, just a seal! It kept on looking at me."

"And no wonder! No damned wonder! Now, leave that monstrosity where it is and I shall break it up for firewood," Mister Keene walked up to the embankment leaving a trail of salt-water in his wake.

Jap ran after him pleading: "If you don't tell Mammy, we will get you some free bottles from the Warren, and we'll not charge you nothing at all."

Mister Keene, our village squire, didn't even turn around to look at him.

Even though I believed that Adolph Hitler had a personal grudge against my father and spent his time roaming the seas in an effort to hunt him down, war was our favourite pastime. Logistics was a relatively simple matter as stones of Cloughey beach served as transport, soldiers, airmen, sailors, ships, planes, tanks and everything else we could think of. The war itself was very much a mixture of the Second World War, the First World War and even the Crimean War but minor skirmishes were for real when my little companions would not abide by recognized international conventions for the conduct of war, for example:

"Who bombed my bridge over the Somme?"

"Uncle Charlie," replied Jap

"It's Uncle Joe, Uncle Joe Stalin! Uncle Charlie is our uncle and he doesn't fly planes like Uncle Joe Stalin does."

"And he's no good at bombing," Teke enforced my argument.

"Who's just blitzed-squeaked Kirkistown Castle? That took me ages to make," moaned young Flint.

"It was Uncle Joe Stallion again," Muddle informed us.
"Uncle Joe, Stupid, Stalin!" How many times have I got to tell you?" I groaned.
"Well I'm going to dam-bust his moat," retorted Flint launching a granite type missile - typical of those times. Within minutes, the area took on a kind of sandy Somme - a look not made any better by Muddle's dog, Flapper, joining in.

Muddle's greyhound, of doubtful pedigree was called 'Flapper' after a flapping track, outside Glasgow from which he was rescued after running in the wrong direction too many times. A flapping track was a greyhound racing track not sanctioned by the controlling body; the National Greyhound Racing Club, where anyone could just turn up with a dog and enter it for a race to be run the same evening. These places were open to all sorts of jiggery-pokery and usually involved poor dogs, bad dogs and even worse dogs. An acquaintance, Jimmy Conan, who worked with me in the Belfast Ropeworks, some thirty years after the above war-games, told me an amusing incident involving a flapping track on the outskirts of Glasgow:
His father was a renowned greyhound trainer and in his kennel, he had an absolute 'flying machine'

that held records both at Dunmore Stadium, Dundalk and Celtic Park. Old Mr Conan (the official trainer) decided to take a short break and left Jimmy, then in his early teens, to feed and look after the dogs in his absence.

The bold, young Jimmy had other plans; he took the champion greyhound on the boat to Stranrear and thereon to the Glasgow flapping track but before entering the stadium he stopped off and rubbed copious amounts of dirt into the glossy coat of the great dog. The dirty dog, held by an equally dirty length of sisal rope fastened to a shabby leather dog-collar approached the official checker:

"What ya call yer dog son?"

"Prince."

"Right! Take Prince over there to get weighed," the checker pointed towards the kennels.

"What's the kennels for?" inquired Jimmy Conan, looking as innocent as he possibly could.

"What's the fucking kennels for? You are new to this game, sonny, aren't you?"

WRONG! Badly, badly wrong! Jimmy had accompanied his father to proper greyhound tracks since he could walk.

He took prices from the bookmakers ranging from, fours, fives, sixes and even sevens in plac-

es all with money he had borrowed from every art and part.
After he had collected his winnings and his dirty dog, he felt a hand on his shoulder:
It was the checker: “If ever you come through that gate again you wee bastard, I’ll stick my boot up both yours and Prince’s arse. Now get that fucking dog back to Ireland or wherever you stole him from.”

My mother came from a village called Ballygowan; which, in Irish, means: ‘The Townland of McGabhann.’ Every year, as children, we went there on holiday to our grandparents’ home and it was there I met a pretty little cousin called Kay, who taught me that playing with girls was much more pleasant than playing with boys, although it has to be said that picking buttercups was less exciting than jumping into the many water-filled quarries in the area (strictly forbidden to us little ones), though she is two years younger than I, she is of my mother’s generation – her father and my grandfather being brothers. Never-the-less she went on to represent her country at bowls and won the ‘Home Countries Championship’ and has warned me that if this fact is not mentioned in my book, she would have my guts for garters.

Ballygowan had a quite successful soccer team. We went to many football matches and on one such occasion, a player kicked the ball mighty high, over the hedge and out of sight. Some of the spectators went to retrieve it but no amount of searching revealed where the 'caser' was. A 'caser' was the name in those days for a leather-covered football and was only affordable by established football teams; the very rich children being bought 'rugger balls'. Little 'eagle eye' Jap knew where the ball was though and casually commented, 'They're looking in the wrong place; the ball bounced over the ditch into the next field.'

"Right, right, right!" I calmed him down, "just shut-up and we'll get it after everybody goes home."

"Think it went into the river and it'll be getting into the sea by now," Teke added, just sufficiently audible to lay a false trail for the caser hunters; for he was street-wise, well beyond his years. After the match, we found it quite impossible to detach ourselves from the Targe, and so I spent a sleepless night wondering if the caser would still be there in the morning.

It was: and it was a real beauty, absolutely new, gleaming with 'Dobbin' and classically finished with a leather lace that could be depended upon to cut the forehead of somebody like me who was never too sure where his head was when trying to connect it with the ball. Finding the football was one thing but getting it from Ballygowan to Cloughey without Mother knowing, was quite another matter altogether. The very first necessity was deflating the monster for in those days it was a much larger football that was used than it is today (size 5 against size 4). Letting the air out was easier said than done, for our little fingers couldn't prize open the leather lacing.

"Anybody got a pin?" I asked.

Teke produced one from a place where a button should have been in his short trousers without too much thought about exposure or the gathering wind. Carefully, I pressed the safety-pin between heavy stitching. Suddenly, there was an almighty crack and the caser took off down the banking like a duck in a drunken stupor.

"Catch it, catch it before it goes into the river," I shouted.

Six skinny wee legs set out after it and caught up with it as it gasped its last breath at the river's edge.

The next problem to be solved was getting it trough Ballygowan village without it being seen. Teke stuffed it up his little 'Fair-Isle' jumper, tried to pat it a bit flatter and smiled.
"You're like a pregnant wee boy," I wasn't at all reassuring.
"Wee boys can't get pregnant," he rebuked.
"It's sticking out too far! Anybody can tell it's a caser. Jap, what is it Teke has stuck up his jumper?"
"A caser."
"See!"
"Could we not hide it somewhere and get it when we are going home tomorrow?" Teke suggested.
"A good idea, but you would still look pregnant tomorrow," I dismissed.
"Sneak it into the portmanteau (large, cloth, carrying bag)" Jap said.
"That's a good idea. We'll take it to the big tree at the Belfast Road and hide it in the branches and then get it when we're going home," I added.

On the morning of departure, the old portmanteau sat bulging in the hallway, but it didn't bulge as much as my eyes when I saw it and realized that it would be one hell-of-a-job getting the caser into it.

"Can I take the portmanteau down to the bus-stop?" I asked Mother.
The Targe looked at me suspiciously: "It's not like you to be volunteering for anything; you haven't been pinching Frame's apples, have you?"
"No, honest, Mammy!"
"Better get Paddy to give you a hand then, it is too heavy for one."
Teke and I struggled, trailed and shunted the heavy bag down the 'Brea' and right on past the bus-stop leaving those standing in the queue a bit gob-smacked. Eventually, we got it hauled to the big tree. Relief! The caser was still there. However, that was only the beginning; we opened the bag and everything inside expanded and bulged out like one of those big tropical flowers you see on television, blooming in slow motion. There was only one solution: Teke and Jap got into the old portmanteau and trampled everything down, whilst I squeezed the caser in.

Having got the precious cargo home, the great bag was left in the bedroom for sorting later but I made sure I was left behind as well – to retrieve the worshipful caser. Again, the contents spilled out and alone, I couldn't quite manage to close the portmanteau.

Some time later there was a sound like a banshee squeal from the bedroom as the Targe discovered the partly opened bag.

"How, in God's name have you got all my clean washing so dirty? Oh Jesus, Mary and Saint Joseph, look at your Granda's tomatoes – bloody well smashed to pieces."

My presence was requested in equally violent tones.

"How in the bloody hell's name have you destroyed everything in this portmanteau?" out mother screamed.

"It burst open and we tried to get everything back in. We tramped on it."

We were severely slapped about and put to bed without supper but if our father had not been at home she would have left us half dead.

On the following day, we tackled the caser. Eventually, we released the leather thong using Vaseline and a hefty pair of pliers. Unfortunately, the inner tube was split; but not to worry, Teke was a dab hand at fixing punctures. He cut a big patch out of an old, bicycle inner-tube and had the caser fixed in no time at all. Little did he know it at the time, but the leather football would wind up with more patches than actual inner tube. Between the old homestead and the Irish Sea there lay a strip of ground, we kids called the 'Strife-acre', but I'm not sure whether the real name should have been 'Strife Acre' or 'Strip Acre' for it was about an acre in size. When us lads were not engaged in household chores we played football there. The usual football was a baldy old tennis ball so when a spanking new leather football was kicked high in the sky it had the effect on our mother of being even more inquisitive than she normally was.

I carried the ball from the field, making sure it was lower down than the myrtle bush so that she couldn't see it from the kitchen window. However, it all was a waste of time, for, as usual; the Targe was a step ahead of me:
"Where the hell's blazes did that ball come from? Who owns it?" She hollered.
"It got washed in with the sea," I lied.
"I swimmed out and got it," Teke added.
"How the hell did you not get wet then?"
"I only swimmed out to my knees."
She made a swipe at each of us as we ran past her.

My brother, the one we called Jap when we were kids had the sharpest eye and the quickest reaction I have ever seen in any human being; for example, in a game of hurling, a player drove the ball at his goal from ten yards out. I had no idea where the ball ended up and assumed it must be in the next field – if not the next parish. He had it in his hand; I couldn't believe my eyes when he side-stepped a couple of attackers and hurled it up the field. Our coach, a man called Davey Bell shook his head and said, "That wee lad will play for his county someday and I'm sure Ulster as well. He never did, for like so many other Irish lads, he fell for the more glamorous game of soccer.

Because of his lightning reaction Jap made for a goalkeeper who was almost unbeatable. Unfortunately, he had a habit of putting his quick reactions to a less popular pastime, and that was: kicking fellows who were much bigger than he was. This habit got me into more trouble than I can remember, for it would have been unthinkable to arrive home with one of my little siblings supporting a 'shiner' if I hadn't caused a bit of GBH to his assailant. Anything short of that would certainly have meant a liberal measure of GBH for me. I didn't mind too much for Father had taught me to box from a very tender age. As long as Jap didn't kick Big Ernie: everything could be sorted out. There was also another one who was a couple of years older than me and consequently, too good for me at the time. We called him 'Cesspit,' and that nick-name suited him in more ways than one for he was a terrible, sectarian bully. Big Ernie's leveller was just around the corner whilst Cesspit would have to wait many years – until I overtook him in height.

Vengeance is not fine wine to be savoured slowly but rather like a rough poteen that will lead to alcoholism of the soul. In my police days, I witnessed a lot of premeditated vengeance and most of it was not nice. An incident of vengeance in which I was the culprit involved a fat man called Pompey who was transferred from a cushy posting to a rough one at Widnes because he upset so many of his colleagues.

On his very first parade, he announced to those of us who were reporting for duty: "If I catch anyone of you stepping out of line, I will book you just like any other member of the public – be warned!"

We had some previous knowledge of this prick, but none of us were prepared for that.

"How to win friends and influence people," I commented.

My good friend, Norman Scott, had to be restrained from levelling him on the spot:

"Abide with me," I advised and I had no intention of singing a hymn.

One evening, Norman was on switchboard duty when he and I hatched a cunning plan:
"Control to 2075," Norman came on the airway.
"Receiving."
"Shea, can you go to 77 Blundell Road, report of a fire."
"Wilco! Is that one of those doss-houses that takes in tramps?" I questioned.
"No it is not! It is my damned house," an excited voice came over the radio. It was Pompey, and he had fallen for our little ploy – hook-line-and sinker.
Five minutes later came this announcement:
"Correction! Correction! The address of that fire should read: 19 Moss Street."
"On my way," I responded.
Another interruption: "That is nowhere near Blundell Road. You two silly bastards are at it. I will have you know that I have a wife and dog in that house. This matter will be reported to the duty inspector."
"Would the person swearing on the radio report to the duty sergeant at once," and it was the duty sergeant on the other end of the line.

From then, until we managed to get rid of him, his life was made a misery but there were only two other incident that I was directly involved in: Simm's Cross was probably the most notorious area of Widnes in the sixties with well over half the drunken brawls occurring there or thereabouts. One night Pompey and I was on patrol just a couple of streets away from there when I heard the sound of shouting and glass smashing. From training days I knew Pompey was a coward and this was my chance:

"Right muscles; let's get around there, that's coming from Simm's Cross."

"I was just about to book all these cars here. None of them have side-lights showing. There have been complaints; they are all customers of that Regency Club you know," he attempted to excuse himself.

"If you do not accompany me, I will report you for dereliction of duty," I shouted at him.

He walked so hesitantly I had to keep pushing him on the back.

"Gets your hands off me, stop pushing me - that is an assault!"

"You will know all about assault when you get around this next corner," I had to yell at Pompey for the din was getting louder.

When we were a good twenty yards off the affray: Pompey stopped, took out his whistle and stood there blasting it as if doomsday had suddenly arrived.
I made my way to those I felt sure were the ringleaders and shouted: “Right you fucking lot: the Black Maria is on its way, and the cells are full of spew already and you will be sharing if you don’t get off-side quickly.”
“Who da fuck?” a big man with a week’s growth of grizzly-beard pushed his way towards me and stuck his face close to mine.
The place got considerably quieter. It was the infamous Gerry McCann, a big Irish man; I had run into before. Gerry was a gentleman when sober and Attila the Hun when drunk.
“Well Jesus God, if it’s not dat bloody Shea again,” he turned to the mob, “If this little fucker tells you to go home you had better listen. Do you hear me?”
One by one the mob drifted away.
“That looked like fraternization," Pompey warned.
“You just shut up!” I jabbed my finger into his fat head.

My final set-up of Pompey involved a ‘drunk and incapable’ or, at least that what Pompey thought a certain Mr Laverty was. If you are prepared to listen, you learn at a very early stage of your career of the two situations to be avoided at all cost;

1. Fishing out dead bodies from the Mersey, when they could be so easily pushed into a current that would take them across to Runcorn and so be dealt with by the Cheshire Constabulary.
2. Arresting drunk and incapable people who will relieve themselves within a few yards of the toilet bowl but never inside it.

In Widnes there lived a man called Laverty: who walked about like a tramp; dressed like a tramp and often sprawled himself out on the pavement, impersonating a person in a drunken stupor. Some say he suffered from fainting fits but I doubt it. There exists certain legislation to deal with impersonation of a police officer but there seemed little need of legislation to deal with the impersonation of drunks. Old Sergeant Nolan pointed Laverty out to me in my early probationary days; informing me that the last time he was arrested it cost Lancashire County Council thousands of pounds for wrongful arrest by the police. Of course, no one was going to tell Pompey that.

One night I was: as usual; somewhere that I shouldn't have been and saw old Laverty lying on the pavement outside the town hall. I quickly returned to where I should have been and got on the radio to the station. Pompey just happened to be covering the town centre beat, which was known as 'A Patrol.'

"I've just had a complaint from a distressed lady who says a man is lying drunk outside the town hall. Could whoever is on that beat deal with it please?"

As long as a drunk was incapable of fighting back, fat Pompey was the man to deal with it but when he summoned the Black Maria, Hughie the Scot, a wise, old-hand, looked at Pompey and uttered: "Are you fucking wise enough, man, that's Laverty the millionaire?"

Pompey did not last long after that. He was dismissed the service for being found patrolling, on night duty, with his Alsatian dog and he not having the authority to do so nor any qualifications as a dog-handler. His biggest problem was fear.

It is one thing trying to rid one's self of a constable but quite another trying to get shut of an inspector but when that horrible, pompous man: DeBrooke, whom I've mentioned before and in similar terminology, got posted to our section, we wondered what we had done to deserve such an insult. One morning I stood at a five road intersection, in the centre of the town, directing traffic. It would have been very obvious to all, but the residents of Rainhill Mental Institute what I was doing, for I had white gloves on that stretched up to my elbows and I was signalling to vehicles which either stopped or proceeded on my command.

"What are you doing now?" this squeaky voice became audible above the noisy traffic. It was Inspector DeBrooke on his first day of supervision.
I tried to simply ignore him, but he persisted:
"What are you doing now?"
"I'm selling fucking ice-cream, Sir!"
Quite suddenly he was not to be seen standing there but it was only minutes before the duty sergeant stood in the exact spot where DeBrooke stood and shouted: "Devaney! Report to the chief inspector's office the minute your traffic duty ends."

Chief Inspector Forsythe was a fine man. Although he stood equally as tall as his namesake; Bruce, he was not the type of man to say: "To see you, to see you, nice."

"PC Devaney! I have a complaint from Inspector DeBrooke to the effect that when you were asked a question, you used the words: "I'm selling fucking ice-cream, Sir!"

"I'm sucking ice-cream, Sir were the actual words I used, Sir"

"You do realize that, even if you used the words you maintain you used it is still the equivalent of telling a superior office to fuck off and that amounts to insubordination?"

"Sorry Sir but I just could not understand how anybody could reach the rank of inspector and not recognise a policeman doing traffic duty."

"Your frivolous attitude toward the job suggests to me that you might be better off as a civilian. Do you appreciate that this matter is a disciplinary one?"

"Yes, Sir!"

"Then you will return to duty and await my decision."

I heard no more about the matter and it might have been down to the fact that I was his 'undercover man' and carried two pocket books, one of which was for his eyes only.

Ronnie Forsythe may have been comparatively lenient on the ordinary beat bobby but when it came to his inspectors, he kept them up to scratch and I sometimes heard them getting a strip ripped off when I was waiting to go in and see him over special operations matters. There was a certain Inspector Herby Costa, who was under so much pressure he eventually had a nervous breakdown. The first I noticed that there was something wrong with him was when he tried to engage me in conversation about the 'Magic Roundabout':

"Dougal is a lot more subtle than Zebedee, don't you think."

"And Ermitrude has a right set tits on her, Sir," I replied thinking it was some kind of a joke.

"That may be so but I was rather intrigued to hear Dougal pull Zebedee about…"

"Yes Sir, but I must be off, if you will excuse me; school crossing patrol in a few minutes."

I am sure he thought I was further around the bend than he was as the time was about eight o'clock in the evening. Things eventually came to a head when he arrived into work one morning in a gleaming tunic, shiny brimmed cap, fine tipstaff and a pair of spotlessly white underpants. Yes, I nearly forgot: he had his shoes on.

One evening we spotted Inspector DeBrooke parked up, at the bottom of Peelhouse Lane, as three of us drove past in a patrol car.

My mate, Fred Smooth was driving and issued the following order to his passengers:
"Everyone open your door and flap it about like we were trying to take off."
We did what we were told and, true to form, the radio crackled into life:
"BD to Z Romeo 415"
"Z Romeo 415 receiving"
"Report from Z Romeo 416 that your car doors are swinging open. Have you a problem - over?"
"Have we a problem, I'd say we have – over."
"Yes 415, what is it? – over."
"Someone had farted – over and out."

Inspector DeBrooke was lead a merry dance at every opportunity. DeBrooke didn't know the town very well and I took advantage of that:
"PC 2075, where are you now," it was time for action when I heard that familiar squeaky voice.
"Outside the Bradley, Sir."
"Where exactly is that?"
"Near Ditton Road, traffic lights, Sir."
"Where is Ditton Road, traffic lights?"
"Widnes Road, Sir"
"And where is Widnes Road?"
"It's in Widnes; where you are now, Sir. I can see you Sir."

I nipped into the nearby entry and watched De-Brooke looking all around for me.

"PC 2075, where exactly, are you now?"

"I'm in the entry, Sir."

"What exactly are you doing in an entry?"

"I'm watching someone acting suspiciously, Sir."

"What is he doing?"

"He is looking all around as if he is casing the joint, Sir"

"What does he look like – this man?"

"He has a little black moustache, a bit like Adolph Hitler, Sir. No, it seems to be alright, Sir. He speaks with a squeaky voice. He must be in some official capacity."

"I shall speak with the man, where, exactly, is he now?"

Whoops! All of a sudden, I was in a bit of a pickle.

"Oh, he has just walked off, Sir."

"Put a report in, to this effect and mention that I was in attendance in a supervisory capacity."

"Oh shit! How am I going to get out of this one?" I thought to myself.

I didn't! I met Chief Inspector Ronnie Forsythe a couple of days later and he pulled me up with the words: "Shea, if you think I have nothing else to do other than read fiction involving Mister De-Brooke then you had better keep in mind there is such a thing as: 'wasting police time - even by other police officers.'

On the subject of wasting time: one of our favourite, childhood playing grounds was 'Charlie's Rocks' situated on the low tide mark in Cloughey Bay. We searched under stones, seaweed and shingle for just anything we could find. It was all a waste of time the day we found what we called a 'gudgie'. I believe the proper name for that fish is a 'gudgeon.' Anyhow it is a small fish with a head on it half the size of your fist and a big mouth that stretches around the best part of the head. The next fish we found was a stickleback. Of course we called it a 'sprick,' well; most of us – Flint called it a 'pwick'.

"Look! Look! I've just caught a pwick," Flint shouted.

"Look, he has; Flint's got a week pwick," Muddle added excitedly.

He had already got it in his small jam-jar, so I suggested putting it in our special storage tank – which was a two-pound jar: the jar containing the big-gobbed gudgie. Within minutes, there was only one fish in the jar; the other was in the big-gobbed gudgie.

"My pwick's gone," Flint moaned.

"The big gudgie must have eaten him," I told him.
"Give me back my pwick," Flint knocked the rim of the jar with a stone, but the gudgie paid little attention.
The rest of the search was quite fruitless but when I called a halt to the session and went to lift the jar, the gudgie was gone. Flapper was sitting beside the knocked over jar with a big smile on his hairy face.
"Flipper, you skinny-assed pig, you've just eaten our gudgie!"
"And my wee pwick that was inside the gudgie, keeping warm," Flint added.

My closest friends will tell you that if I get into a fit of laughing, it is difficult to get me out of it. I have no time for slapstick, a little time for situational comedy and a lot of time for subtle and satirical humour. Twice I was thrown out of court for laughing. Both times several other policemen were thrown out with me but on those occasions, it was completely different policemen who were involved, which might tend to give the impression that I started it off.

In Widnes Magistrate's Court, a little man by the name James Hatton was called for:

"Call James Hatton."

"James Hatton," the court usher repeated.

A little man walked into the courtroom. His head was much too large for his body, which, in turn was much too small for his ears. He was so comical looking that, later in life, I used him as one of my characters: 'Jonas Gulpspider,' in my book of humour, called 'Plonkton.' But what really started me off laughing was: he still had his flat cap on. The court usher came rushing in after the little man, grabbed the cap from his head and, with a red scowling face, handed it to the owner. It was obvious that James Hatton was a tad deaf and hadn't heard the usher ask him to remove the cap as he entered the court. However, the really funny thing was: the little man thanked the court usher and promptly put the cap back on. I presumed that the silly little twit thought he had left it on the bench in the waiting room and that the usher was returning it to him.

"Would you please remove your cap whilst in this courtroom," the magistrate's clerk demanded in a loud voice.

At first, Hatton did nothing but realizing everyone was looking at him, pointed at himself, shook his narrow shoulders, pointed at his cap and only then did he remove it from his head.

James Hatton was shown to the witness box and the magistrate's clerk commenced swearing him in:

"Raise the bible in your right hand and repeat the words after me."

The little man raised his flat cap in his right hand.

"Mister Hatton, I distinctly said: 'bible' yet you appear to have raised your cap!"

"Sorry, Your Worship," said he, raising the bible in his right hand – after he had put on his flat cap again.

"Mister Cappon .. err .. Mister Hatton; remove that cap!" the magistrate's clerk was running out of patience.

I was so far gone at this stage I sounded like a braying donkey in a dark forest looking for a mate. The majority of the policemen sitting beside appeared to be rocking form side to side.

The chairman of the bench, a respected Conservative got to his feet:

"Would the policemen, who think these proceedings are a laughing matter, please remove themselves from my court," he demanded, pointing the culprits out, one by one. I was the first he pointed at.

I spent the next half hour parading up and down the waiting-room chanting to myself: "When it is

my turn to go in there I will not laugh! It is not funny! I will not laugh."
It didn't work and one again I found myself in front of Chief Inspector Forsythe.

The second time I was put out of court was for something even funnier. This middle-aged lady, with plenty of war-paint on, got into the witness box:
"And what is your name, madam?" the magistrate's clerk asked her.
"Ophelia."
"Ophelia what?"
"Dicks"
"Ophelia Dicks!" the magistrate's clerk had to cover his mouth and turn slightly away from our view until he recovered sufficiently.
But it was too late; I had burst out again into my familiar donkey impression taking half the police constables with me. This time it was a lady 'chair-person' on the bench. She too was a leading Conservative in the town and completely devoid of humour.
A lot of uniformed men found themselves ejected from the court and for my part at least, once again in front of Ronnie Forsythe:
"Devaney, do you take any aspect of this job seriously."

"Of course, Sir, why just the other day .."

"Cut the bullshit; just give me your account of events," the Chief Inspector interrupted me.

"Well Mister Forsythe, it was like this: the magistrate's clerk asked this old girl what her name was and she replied: 'Ophelia.' 'Ophelia what? says he?' 'Dicks: says she.'"

"Ophelia Dicks!" the Chief Inspector gasped.

"Yes, Sir – Ophelia Dicks!"

"You mean to tell me that parents by the name of Dicks actually called their daughter Ophelia?" With that he burst out laughing, swiped a wave of his hand and demanded: "Get out of here, Devaney."

Another incident, involving a court – actually a high court – I did not find funny at the time: I was summoned unexpectedly from holiday in Ireland to attend the high court in Liverpool in my other role of divisional draughtsman. A police escort picked me up from the cross-channel ferry early in the morning but the case was postponed to the afternoon so my escort and I retired to a pub for a spot of 'brunch' and a few beers of course. By the time I was called, I was half-full: tripped on the second step of the witness box sending my plans everywhere, including unto the distinguished Judge Oppenshaw's bench.

The great man simply glanced at me and asked:
"Officer is this the way you normally present your plans to the court?"
He was noted for his humour; at one time, having sentenced an' incorrigible rogue' – as persistent criminals were once called – to ten years; the old lag pleaded: "Your Worship, I could never do all that time."
"Well, do as much as you can," Oppenshaw advised.

The job as the divisional draughtsman involved going on a course to a training unit at headquarters in Preston. Whilst I was there a firm was employed to carry out a pipe laying scheme, which meant digging a trench across a nearby field. Four men turned up one morning and we watched as they commenced digging the trench. The man in charge of the drawing department, a certain Sergeant Hoskins, a terrific gentleman, said to me: "What do you bet me that those four aren't countrymen of yours?"
"Why do you say that?"
"The speed they are going at, look, they have dug about ten yards in half-an-hour. Now, no Englishman is daft enough to actually work as fast as he can."

I was not convinced and bet him two bob, but a couple of hours later I was not so sure. By that time they had extended the trench half way across the field.
Sergeant Hoskins shook his head as he peered out of the window: “I do think they are digging in the wrong direction.”
“That bet’s off,” I interrupted.
The sergeant left the office but returned later with the news that his assumption was right: they were; all four, Irishmen and they had, in fact, spent several hours digging a trench in the wrong direction.
“Do you know what the boss-one said when the error was pointed out to him?” Hoskins could hardly speak for laughing.
“No, what?”
“He said, ‘Dat will be alright, Sir. We will speed things up a bit, Sir and have it put right in an hour or so.”
“What’s so funny about that?” I asked.
“They were slacking it a bit,” he bent over double laughing at his own joke.

On the subject of Englishmen/Irishmen: A long time after the above incident, I was at Earl’s Court attending a show when an English drunk begged money off me for ‘a cup of tea.’

Without speaking I handed him a pound coin.
"Thanks Paddy," he bowed his head.
"How did you know I was Irish?"
"An Englishman never gives anyone a pound, Sir."
"Well there you are then, now don't go spending it on something to eat; get yourself something substantial like a bottle of cider," I suggested.

Mother was quite a proud person and tried to give others the impression that we were a cut above them, and this was no more so evident than parading us up to the front pew in our parish church. Mount St Joseph Church was built on a hill, as might well be derived from its name. The hill wasn't so high as to have caused problems to the few cars which were around in those days, provided they had brakes, that is. Another status quo element was: arriving by taxi, but that is where the question of brakes comes into the equation. There is little point swelling into the church from a taxi that has no brakes. You just become a laughing stock.
"Do we get Jim Morrison's taxi cheaper because it has bad brakes," I put the question to our mother, but got no reply, which was a good indication that the question should not be repeated.

The real story is: if we got behind another car or someone walked across our path Jim Morrison's taxi careered back down the hill and right across the road winding up with its ass stuck in Charlie Murray's hedge. In such incidents praying started before entering the church:
"Jesus, Mary and Saint Joseph, we're all going to be killed," the Targe woman, would yell, whilst us three young lads thought it was quite thrilling.
Jim Morrison wasn't as thrilled as we were as he went around the back of the taxi and trailed branches and shrubs from around the wheels, he was heard to mutter: "Jesus, Mary and Saint Joseph, would you just look at the state of this." Now that was something coming from Jim, who was a protestant that could well have been asked to hand in his Orange Order sash for such forbidden language.

School confessions on one particular day took on a serious tone indeed, for huddled together; in St Joseph's church doorway were three 'little men' who had a very guilty secret to dilute somewhat before presenting it to the parish priest – Father William Walsh – in return for absolution and the opportunity to do the same thing all over again. It was the infamous, 'Jumping Stone' plot.

According to our Paddy, who was not much fussed on being called Teke at this stage in his life, and his two pals Eddie and Seamus, a little brook at the end of McCarthy's Lonnen contained a magic stone, one that amazingly hopped out of the water without the assistance of any human being, or anything else – for that matter. But, like many such privileges, there were conditions attached; any young maidens, wishing to witness the great phenomena, had to submit themselves to a medical examination by three grossly unqualified practitioners. The candidates were carefully selected and suitably persuaded to, at least, go to the little brook. Whether any stone actually jumped they do not say but we are left to believe the young maidens' honour remained intact for they were heard running back up the guttery lane screaming.

But there was one place the whole episode would have to come to light in and that was: the confessional box and that was not a comforting prospect for 'jumping stones,' for the want of a better phrase, was the top sin in the Catholic Church in those days and for many more days to come. It rated a classification of 'mortal' and carried the dreaded punishment of everlasting burning of human flesh in the hells of eternal damnation –

which renders the phrase ‘chilling prospect’ rather inappropriate in this case. And so: the reason for the three little men huddling together in the church doorway.

“No! I’m too scared to tell him about the jumping stones thing, “Seamus insisted.

“But we have to tell him it too,” Paddy tried to reassure him.

“No, I’m not going in!”

“Here’s what you can do,” Paddy has a cunning plan, “You write down your sins, all of them and Eddie can give them to Father Walsh when he’s going in.”

“Am I allowed to do that but?” Eddie wasn’t too sure.

Paddy patted the latter on the back: “Lots of big people does that when they are away at sea and things. They send their confessions back by Royal Mail.”

The trio were huddled over a grubby jotter page and a stubby pencil for the next fifteen minutes:

“No, you can’t put that! Don’t mention ‘knickers'," Paddy advised, and a dirty, crumbled rubber erased the forbidden word.

“That’ll do,” an impatient Seamus handed over the confession to Eddie.

"No, you'll have to sign it or Father Walsh will think I did it twice," Eddie handed the paper back for the required signature.
With that: three little short-trouser clad young boys scurried back into the church.
When it came Eddie's turn he must have tried to fulfil his task for; after some, lengthy whispering, the priest was heard to say: "Edward, why don't you just tell Seamus to bring that sheet of sins into me – himself?"

The three little men talked about above were altar-boys. One Sunday morning they forgot to fetch out the big brass bell which had to be rung at the most important part to the service – the raising of the host.
"There's no bell! The bell's not there," Paddy informed Seamus.
"It's Eddie that's supposed to ring it, today," Seamus retorted.
"Tell him to shout: 'Ding-a-ling-a-ling' when he should be ringing the bell."
Some whispering and nodding of little heads took place. Father Walsh raised the leavened bread but there was a conspicuous couple of second's pause then:
"Ding-a-ling-a-ling," a thin little voice broke the silence.

"Eddie, just go and fetch the bell, son!" the priest instructed.
As they left the sacristy a man, we always called 'The Doc', although he had no medical qualifications, slid towards the little boys, grinning: "My Ding-a-ling-a-ling, My Ding-a-ling-a-ling, I'd like you to play with My Ding-a-ling-a-ling." It should have been a warning but in those days any mention of such impropriety would not have been entertained by anyone.

The banter must have gone on far too long for on one of those special days when the church has a procession down the aisle, Paddy decided to take ecclesiastical law into his own hands – fingers to be more accurate. It was not quite a candle-light possession but one in which the lead alter-boy lights the candle of the end-man in the pew with a burning wax taper. That man then passes the light, candle-touch by candle-touch, down the pew. Anyhow, the Doc got his wick-end lit and was just about to pass on the 'sacred flame' when another alter-boy in the possession reached out with wet fingers and snuffed out his candle. Jay Tourney thought it was hilarious, so he got the same treatment. My brother must have enjoyed the attention he was getting for he then decided to do most of the remaining candles on his way down. There never was so much fuss, bustling, fizzling, spitting and striking of matches ever seen before or since in the Church of Mount Saint Joseph.

The Doc was a regular visitor to Rubane House, an orphanage run by the Christian brothers where it has been discovered that abuse of boys was endemic. We used to play hurling against those children and on one such outing, a little black boy called Massa, took my brother aside and whispered:
"Paddy, if only you knew what they do to us in that place," pointing to the big house.
None of us understood what that child spoke of, but one thing is for sure: had we known, there was no chance of us telling our mother for she would have beaten us stupid as she did with me when I drew a man with a dog's head. It is all down to the Church and their twisted sense of morality. The visiting, so-called 'missionaries' would go red in the face with anger when thundering against sex outside marriage whilst engaged in brutal paedophilia with their masters turning a blind eye often as the result of fearing personal accusations for similar offences in days gone by. How anyone can torture a little, innocent child, for their own evil gratification is sim-

ply beyond comprehension. With the Church's history of usury, instigating wars, torture and covering up paedophilia is it little wonder Jesus is said to have sweated blood in the Garden of Gethsemane.

I wrote earlier of my dread of having to face Big Ernie and Cesspool. The laws of chance would indicate that it had to happen sooner or later – in the case of Big Ernie: sooner! The fact that we suddenly were the proud owners of a big, new caser stacked the odds against me avoiding such confrontation, as the kids from all over the village descended on the strife-acre to get a game with a real football. No one of the village kids would have had the courage to come to the door looking for us, or should I say 'looking for the caser', as the Targe would have seen them off in no time. As a result, they played with a spongy thing, still global shaped in a number of places but with lumps missing, until such time as I arrived carrying the caser.

Unfortunately, the bigger the crowd of kids: the greater the chance of trouble and many a match ended with fists flailing. As I have stated before it was my number-one duty to protect my two siblings and generally, I took it in my stride and we all parted with no more damage done than a bleeding nose or busted lip. Big Ernie was a head taller and a good foot wider than I and had a reputation for 'taking no nonsense.' He was hopeless at football whilst our little Jap was brilliant. Big Ernie was brilliant at one thing though: knocking the living daylights out of anyone who was better than him at football.

In the middle of the match, I heard a weird moaning jumbled with the words: "Ma balls, ma bloody balls: that wee bastard just kicked me in the bollocks."

"Oh, my God!" I thought, "that sounds like Big Ernie – I just hope the 'wee bastard is not our Jap." It was!

As I gingerly made my way to the scene of the disaster Big Ernie stopped rolling in agony and sat on his fat ass – which put me on equal terms with him – height wise.

"That fucking bastard! That wee bastard brother of yours, has done my stones in." Big Ernie was alternating his glare between my little brother and his swelling scrotum.

"He couldn't have kicked you in gools, Big Ernie; he couldn't reach up that high with his foot on them wee, short legs. It must have been someone else," I ventured.

With that statement, the players of both teams pointed fingers at my brother whilst getting off-side themselves. For a brief moment, I pictured Big Ernie getting to his feet and flailing me alive with his big mitts; not to mention his outsized feet but, against that, I pictured the Targe beating me with a shovel or a brush handle until I could longer feel the pain.

I made my decision: “Which of your stones did he kick you on, Big Ernie?”

“What does it matter which bollock he got me on?” he replied, looking down, no doubt to make sure they were still attached.

With that: I went over and kicked Big Ernie in the same place but I couldn’t swear as to which stone I connected with.

“You bastard! You bastard! You lousy, fucking bastard,” Big Ernie bellowed, yelled and howled, grabbing his testicles, rolling around and flipping about like a monster fish recently landed on a river bank.

“If you try to get up I will kick you again,” I warned Big Ernie.

“Get him off me, somebody get him off me,” he yelled, doing his best to roll away from my threat-ening boot.

I took that as an admission of defeat and hurried-ly grabbed the caser and the two young ones; in that order of priority and escorted them over of our myrtle hedge and the safety of the old homestead.

As far as kicking was concerned: justice was seen to be done some fifteen years later when, in the police, I was sent to a miner's house in Ditton. No one had though to tell me but the preferred way to settle disputes amongst northern miners is to have a kicking bout, in which, the last man standing on sound legs is the winner. The little man must have been all of fifty years of age.
"Right, I'm arresting you for causing a breach of the peace," I cautioned the little man.
"You just think you are," he replied.
In the next minute or so he had lifted lumps of flesh out of my shins and knees with his hobnailed boots. I had to get to the back of the short miner, and quickly, in order to avoid those lashing boots. I think I got a further kick on the ass as I executed my move. Anyhow, I managed to get around the back of the little bugger, grabbed him by the head – only to find out he had a head on him like a concrete block. I found it difficult to keep a grip on his slippery nut but luckily for me; his age caught up with him and he collapsed panting for breath.

"It's the coal dust," he panted and talked to me as if I was someone he was having a pint with, "I'll be alright in a minute or two." I think he was asking me to let him have a rest so that he could resume the contest.
I snapped handcuff on him: "Look mate, I've no intention of waiting on Raymond Barrington Dolby's inter-round summaries - get these on you!"

In those days policemen were not nearly as restricted by rules, regulations and codes of practice as they are today. There was an unspoken requirement, and it was: "Thou shalt not let your colleagues down when the going gets tough." Unfortunately, for Ronnie Forsythe and his like: it was usually the dependable who were the greatest nuisances in the long run. The first example of that theory is: Two of us went into Ditton sub-station, which had recently closed down and searched through it to see what we might unearth.
"Ah!" I exclaimed, "What's this?" taking a strange object down from a dusty old cupboard.
"I know what that is," my Scottish colleague informed me.
"What is it then?"
"It's an old air-raid siren; see that handle on it? That's for winding round and round. It makes a

hell of a noise. Don't wind it unless you want to waken up everybody on this side of Liverpool. That gave me an idea:

Ten minutes later we were in the middle of Dundalk Road waste ground with the big siren. I wound it up to a mighty speed. The sound was deafening.

"Right, stop it Shea! That sound is literally driving me mad. Put it back in the car and let's be off."

A short time later every patrol was asked as to their whereabouts and informed about several reports of an air-raid siren being set off. The duty inspector and sergeants were all relatively new to the section and would not have known about the existence of the old siren. But Sergeant John Mossop wasn't new and the next day he cast a suspicious eye over my colleague and I as he related the tale that, on hearing the sound, several old war veterans had jumped out of their beds; some searching for uniforms, some hiding in cupboards and under beds, others calling out for directions to the nearest air-raid shelter and one old man was found in his underpants running up Hale Road shouting, "The bloody Huns are back."

In those early days, policemen were expected to provide their own bicycles for use in outlying beat patrols. Shortly before the incident that I am about to relate, I had purchased a new green Raleigh bicycle of the 'sit-up-and-beg' generation and I was 'right proud of it' as they would say in Lancashire, so proud, in fact, that I named him 'Sir Walter.' It was handy to be on a bicycle when some of your mates were getting it big time at Simms Cross. Amongst the most troublesome and obnoxious people, I have ever had to deal with were Fred James and Piggy O'Rourke and if I was asked to pick the worse of the two it would have to be Piggy. Whoever named him 'Piggy' must have been one of those 'Best of breed' judges at an agriculture shows for he strongly resembled a British saddleback but was not quite as tasty. One night I got a call that Piggy was kicking a steel wastepaper bin around the street, now-and-again, picking it up and throwing it at passing cars. A young recruit was trying to reason with O'Rourke, from the side of the kerb, when I arrived on my trusty stead; 'Sir Walter.'

"Get off the road, you fucking idiot," I shouted, thinking it might be better to appeal to a person's better nature than use persuasive tactics.

"Get to fuck, out of here before I kick your fucking head in with my football here," was the reply that I based the judgement on; that he was not prepared to consider my request.

"Alright, Piggy, but I believe you are about to cause an accident," and I cycled off leaving the young recruit with his mouth hanging open. I went up Grenfell Street and back down the Widnes Road. Piggy was standing in the centre of the road with his back towards me. I picked up a bit of speed and drove my bicycle right between his legs, knocking him arse over tit unto the roadway.

"I did warn you that you might cause an accident," I told him as a couple of his mates trailed him to the side:

"Come on Piggy, them bastards are just trying to wind you up," I heard; in what might be described as the understatement of the year.

It is difficult to say where I should have been on the particular day I am going to write about, but I remember where I was; that being Mersey Road, which was part of 'B Patrol.' As I was cycling, on a lovely sunny day, a lorry came around a corner and a load of empty beer-barrels went tumbling off it. Some bounced, some rolled and some levelled anything in their pathway. Other such 'weapons of mass-destruction', headed in my direction at an amazing speed. I zigzagged, from one side of the road to the other avoiding as many as I possibly could. Unfortunately, one got me. It pinned the front wheel of 'Sir Walter' up against road railings bending both beyond recognition.

The lorry stopped, and the young driver walked towards me: "Sorry Officer, have I punctured your bike?"

"Have you punctured my bike? You nearly fucking killed me, you daft bastard!"

"If you don't say anything about that, I'll plead guilty to 'an insecure load,' the young driver: Eddie Myatt suggested.

"What about my new bicycle, the front wheel is wrecked?"

"If you bring it to my house, up in Avondale Drive, I will fix it up for you as good as new."

"I'm not going to walk three miles with a busted bike over my shoulder like some Irish prick that's just come off the cattle boat."

"I can throw it on the lorry and take it with me."

"Only to have it fly off at the first corner you go around like a flaming bat out of hell."

"Here, look, I'll let you hold this watch as a guarantee, the driver began taking a watch off his wrist, "It might not be as valuable as your bike, but I can't do without it."

Eddie Myatt, had a wonderfully jolly face and appeared quite genuine, for the criminal he certainly was, so I agreed to the fixing of the bicycle; without holding his watch. From that day onward he, not only became my friend, but was affectionately known, within our circle, as 'Odd Jobs Myatt.'

Odd Jobs Myatt came in useful when a young police constable, originally from Bolton, got into his patrol car and drove it backwards just as I was driving my patrol car forwards; with the inevitable result. The damage wasn't excessive, so I knocked up Eddie about 3am and we all headed off to a garage where Odd Jobs knocked out the dents and sprayed the damaged areas. It wasn't likely that we would get a call at that time in the morning and that is how it worked out. The maintenance sergeant was rather suspicious, when he went to repair an earlier prang, that had been reported, to the 'area car' – the one I had been driving and found that the dent had miraculously disappeared.

Up until the dramatic end of my police career, I often called in with Eddie for a cup of tea. Most of the time; his back door was unlocked. If he had a 'skin-full' I wouldn't bother waking him up but just helped myself. It was on such an occasion that I opened the back door, put the kettle on, spread the morning paper out on his table and went upstairs to the toilet. I couldn't help noticing that there was smoke coming from his room, so I assumed Eddie was at home. I pushed the door open and saw him lying there, as happy as Larry, with the bed on fire. Actually, it was smouldering and glowing brightly on the patch where he had dropped his lit cigarette. If his window had not been opened, blowing the smoke out of the room, he would have been a goner.

"You could get yourself a gong for this," Eddie suggested when he sobered up, "Maybe promotion?"

"Yea, yea, and what was I supposed to be doing here eh? More likely that mob down there would write us off as a couple of woofters."

Needless-to-say, with all the goings-on, I became quite infamous, not just in 'R Division' but throughout the force and got blamed for many incidents, which had nothing to do with me. As the divisional draughtsman I visited head-quarters more than the average cop. One day as I was sitting in the canteen I overheard a PC talking to a sergeant in a voice that was too loud to ensure

privacy over the distance between them and I. Perhaps I was meant to hear it:
"There he was smoking away and when he had finished he threw the butt on the stairs. Unfortunately, for him, the Super was following him and shouted: 'Devaney is that your fag?' 'You can have it, you saw it first, Sir' replied the bold Shea," related the PC and they both broke into howls of laughter. If that could happen within my hearing: how many other tales have been made up about me? I think that if the tale was worth telling and they forgot the name of the culprit, they just pinned it on me.

The first school we attended, as infants, was Ballyphillip Primary and if a rougher, tougher school ever existed, it must have been in Kirby, Huyton or Widnes. Playtime brought no respite from the violence of the class-room for immediately after eating our jam sandwiches the 'The War' started. Sometimes it started even earlier; depending upon whether or not the poorest children had anything to eat. I suppose when compared to the battle for Stalingrad or the fire-bombing of Essen and Dresden, it was mild enough, but at the time it could be very frightening. Weapons consisted of sticks, stones, penknives, well-worn kitchen knives and monstrous bits of steel with handles secured with wrapped string. The most terrifying weapon of all was the burning whin-bushes (gorse to the non-Gaelic). One child actually was shot in the forehead with an air-pistol but the slug didn't enter the skull. Being taken prisoner was to be avoided at all costs as jail was the putrid-smelling dry-toilet. Few prisoners attempted escape as the punishment was; having one's head rammed down one of the communal lavatory holes (open trench toilets). Is it any wonder I was fleet of foot?

On reaching the age of eleven each of us, in turn were transferred to Ballycran Public Elementary School which had a better educational rating. At that school, we had a very brilliant, academic headmaster but he was an alcoholic. When he went on leave he inevitably returned late and during his drying out period he was cruel: slapping little children because they simply did not know an answer to some question he asked. At school I have been slapped with a heavy, brutal, black strap until my hands were completely numb and then slapped again for not being able to hold a pencil between my swollen fingers and thumb. The class-rooms were very poorly heated and on frosty days the worst pain of all was the feeling returning to numbed hands after such beatings. I remember wishing that the numbness would remain if only I could get to grips with the pencil. In those days, justice could not be found for children in the State, the Church or the home – any form of complaint would be quickly quelled through further violence.

One particular strapping: I brought on myself. Music lessons meant one thing and one thing only; the singing of 'The Rose of Mooncoine' and 'Joe the Carrier Lad' and it was all down to the fact that they were songs associated with County Cork, where the headmaster hailed from. I became rather bored with the whole thing and decided to spice the latter song up a bit:
The line; 'My horse is always willing and I am oh, so glad' became:
'My horse is always dunging and I am oh, so sad.'
I acted like a seasoned ventriloquist not moving my lips as I sang. Every time: at that line, everyone started laughing and the headmaster was at his wits end as to who was doing it for; if he came too close I simply sang the correct line. My position for singing was in the back row with all the rest of the tone deaf. One particular day he instructed us to sing: 'Joe the Carrier Lad' and to sing it again when we had finished it. He then announced he would be leaving for five minutes.

He went out and around to the back of the school to the window, he had conveniently opened, which was right behind where I stood.
He returned, amidst the uproar and quietly sang: "My horse is always dunging and I am oh, so sad."
Silence prevailed.
Then he shouted, "Devaney come to the front of the class."
He let me stand there for a time contemplating my punishment then asked me to turn around and face the class: "Now sing; 'Joe the Carrier Lad' – from start to finish," he instructed.
That was the main course; I had a couple of slaps for desert but why he had to punish the whole class by making them listen to my singing is beyond me.

Just before my brother James transferred to Ballycran Public Elementary School he dashed into the house to announce: "Mammy, Mammy, I've just seen an old woman swallow her neck.
"Don't talk nonsense," the Targe chastised, "How could she swallow her neck, unless she has a trunk like a bloody elephant?"
It intrigued me so much that I asked everyone I came upon as to who it could possibly be. The favourite turned out to be Lena Ferron. I kept a

beady eye on her every time I had the opportunity.

I eventually got caught gazing at her:

"What ye looking at ye wee gob-shite," she screamed at me as I concentrated on her every mouth movement.

Granted, she always appeared as if she was chewing her cud but I had to wait a long time to witness her 'swallowing her neck.' Then it happened; I was travelling home on a bus from Portaferry, after having a haircut. Lena Ferron got on the bus at her home in the tiny village of Newcastle.

"It's you, you wee staring gob-shite again," she screeched, on spying me, putting her mouth under the microscope again.

I noted that she was completely toothless; with a top lip that protruded much further than her tiny chin. Then it happened; what I had been patiently waiting for; she wrapped her floppy top lip down over her tiny, hairy chin.

"So that's what Jap means by 'swallowing her neck,'" I nodded to myself in a sense of satisfaction.

You have no doubt heard of many an explorer endeavouring to discover the source of great rivers; well, we went the opposite way and arranged an expedition to discover where the 'Main Drain' entered the sea. The Main Drain is situated about a mile from where we used to live. We knew exactly where it went underground but had no idea where it went after that. One day the 'Infamous Five' decided that it was time to solve the mystery and armed with a flash-light, smuggled out of his house by Muddle, we headed off in our great expedition. We had no trouble squeezing through the bars where the little brook went underground. After walking some distance we came across rusty old steps that lead to a manhole cover. Teke ascended the steps but I had to go up behind him for it took the two of us to prise open the cover.

"Fucking hell!" was all I heard, from someone who was obviously startled by the cover rising up and the appearance of just four little eyes out of the darkness.

We did not wait to find out who it was nor did the startled man remove the cast-iron lid.

The iron culvert pipe gets bigger as it nears the shore and that had the effect of magnifying our voices like some big powerful megaphone so, it should have been no surprise to find a motley mixture of whelk pickers, tourists and day trippers awaiting our exit.

"Doctor Livingston, I presume," a tall slender man with a handlebar moustache and dressed in green tweed joked.
I didn't have a clue as to who Doctor Livingston was, so I answered: "There's only Doctor Duff or Doctor Young, who fixes people here."
"Do you know Mister Keene?" inquired Flint.
I didn't know why Flint asked the tall man that, but on reflection; I suppose he did look like someone who should have known Mister Keene or, perhaps, he was simply name dropping for his own protection.
"No, I do not know your Mister Keene but what I do know is that you would all have been trapped had the sea come in," the man in tweed cautioned.
"The tide hasn't even reached Charlie's Rocks yet," I replied with authority, for we may not have known anything about Doctor Livingston but there was nothing a visitor could tell us about the Irish Sea.

Since a very tender age, I've had a problem with that old character we called the 'Devil.' I just couldn't imagine how a person could reside in a fiery hell and be none the worse off for it. Would he have burns all over his body or would he be so badly burned that he would be totally black?

It couldn't be Uncle Tom from 'Uncle Tom's Cabin' as he could sit down without hurting himself overmuch, and he was a kind man and the devil certainly was not. Then someone came along to fit the bill, albeit, with the inappropriate name of 'Bishop McCarthy.' It was rumoured that McCarthy fought a priest in the sacred sanctuary of the church:

"Do you realize I am a priest!" the loser complained.

"Aye and I'm a bishop!" the victor retorted and that was how Bishop McCarthy was supposed to have acquired his title.

In regards to Bishop McCarthy: other rumours circulated around the school children; things such as 'possession; horns and prowling at night in a red cape whilst carrying a trident.' The truth was an anti-climax: We decided to scrump apples from his orchard, totally confident that he did not awake until it went dark. We were right about one thing; he was, indeed, asleep when we spied him under an apple tree, but he had a glorious smile on his face as if he was totally at ease with creation. From that moment onwards I began questioning the things I had been told; things, that up until then, I held sacrosanct.

Before I leave the subject of 'the Devil' it might be interesting to know that I, as a very young boy thought that the Devil visited Mrs Gillis' pump-house and left his special smells there. It was my job, as the eldest, to make sure that the big, white enamel bucket was filled with drinking water each night before I went to bed. I had this particular job before I was truly able to lift the full bucket off the pump spout. As a result, some of the water spilled over as I attempted to lift it down but if there was too much spilt I was sent immediately back to get a full bucket. It took me a long time to catch on that I need not bring what was left in the bucket back to the pump for a top-up and so reduce the risk of my skinny wee legs become wet and cold, especially on frosty nights. The worst situation for someone so small was to find that the pump needed priming either through being iced up or air-locked. I had to slide the great iron 'bonnet' as I called it far enough to the side to get some rain-water into the pump to encourage it to start. Sometimes the pump-house contained some weird smells. It turned out that the smells were caused by an old woman called Annie Bailey, who was employed to clean Mrs Gillis' house. She smoked Turkish cigarettes in there when she could afford them and tea-leaves when she couldn't, but my vivid imagination put it down to visits from the old Devil himself.

The second job I had to perform at night was to fill the coal-bucket. There were no coal scuttles to be found in poor houses in those days. My mother was wise enough to realize she couldn't afford for me to be afraid in the dark, so she explained every noise I encountered; from barking badgers to the moaning of the old fog-horn and sights from flying bats to scavenging rats. Banshees, she explained was nothing more than dogs howling in the darkness. Therefore, it was no surprise to her when I bounced a lump of coal off a large 'white apparition' which turned out to be my father, dressed up in a white sheet, who had returned home during my nightly chores and 'appeared' from behind Daddy Adair's garage.

"What did it sound like?" my father asked after the commotion.

"It sounded like some big man pretending to be a ghost," I replied but couldn't understand why my parents thought that answer was very funny.

I don't think I would ever have qualified as 'Santa's little helper' for I was not the greatest messenger boy in Cloughey. As a matter of fact, I could easily have been the worst for my mind was always on more interesting things, notwithstanding, that to return with the wrong item would inevitably mean a 'foot in the ass' or worse. A typical example might be; being sent for 'a black spool number 40' and returning with 'a yard of white bias-binding.'

On one particular occasion in which I did arrive back with a black spool number 40 instead of a pan loaf the Targe bounced the black spool number 40 off my nut shouting: "A black spool number shit! You get back in there and bring me back what I asked for."

I was in no more informative a position when I returned to Mrs Gillis other than knowing for sure that a black spool number 40 was not required on that particular day.

"Maybe son, it's a white spool number 40," Mrs Gillis suggested, comforting me by patting my little fair head, "What exactly did your mammy say?"

"A black spool number - shit!" I looked back over my shoulder as I spluttered out the bad word.

"No it would hardly be that. Perhaps it's a yard of black bias-binding," Mrs Gillis suggested, again comforting me by patting my head, "What do you think, son?"

"Yes that is what it is: a yard of black bias-binding," I nodded.

As I neared our front door, I felt a little less confident and it was a correct feeling as it turned out, "How the hells, bloody blazes, am I going to feed a family on a yard of bloody, black bias-binding?" my mother howled attacking me as I tried to escape.

There was not much in the police code of conduct that I held sacrosanct and that attitude often got me into trouble with my superiors. At other times, I got into trouble through sheer chance and circumstance. And there were times where I should have been in trouble that I often got off scot-free. Every time I hear that old song, 'Burning Bridges,' one such incident comes to mind:

One bright and sunny afternoon I was on 'B Patrol' and strangely enough, that is where I was supposed to be. I walked down a pathway that led from Lugsdale Road to the canal. As I walked under an iron footbridge that connected two parts of I.C.I. property, I noticed that three burly men were in the process of burning it down with oxyacetylene gear.

"Have you got a light, Sir? This burner keeps going out in the wind up here," a man with an Irish accent asked me.

I climbed up and supplied them with a few matches and was soon on my way again without giving it any more thought.

The following morning the duty sergeant read out a list of incidents and asked: "Who was on B Patrol yesterday?"

"I was." I replied.

"You will be surprised to hear that someone nicked a complete footbridge belonging to the I.C.I. Why did you not discover it, Shea?"

"Too busy to go to those outlying places; anyhow, the I.C.I. is private property. They have their own security."

"Yes, I'm told there are a few people in trouble in that department."

Another happening in that same I.C.I. property occurred in a large, disused engine shed. When we were on the night shift, we used to drive our patrol cars in there to have a fag or two and to discuss, women, horses and what we had in store for Pompey or DeBrooke. We always drove in on side-lights so as not to draw any attention to ourselves. On the particular night of the occurrence, three of us met up at 3am. On parade at 10pm the following night the duty sergeant informed us that a man had been found hanged in that same shed. Sometime later a post-mortem showed that he had died between 1am and 3am. Assuming he did not come into the engine shed and do himself in whilst we were smoking away in one of the cars; he must have been swinging above us without us having a clue he was up there.

In our young days hens were everywhere and it was a common sight to see them being 'shooed' out of kitchens and sculleries. Muddle had a theory on hens that the other four of us found hard to understand:

"If you put two Willie-hens together they will fight until one of them is dead," he told us as we gazed at Aggie Brown's flock of brown hens.

"I've never seen a Willie-hens in my life, show me one in them there hens," I asked him.

"There, over there, that big one, that's a Willie-hen."

"That's a rooster. A rooster is a daddy-hen."

"No! My uncle Jamsie says it's a Willie-hen."

"Maybe he meant a woolly hen," Flint suggested.

"I never seen a woolly hen either. Maybe he was looking at a sheep eh?" I tried to help Muddle out.

"No! My uncle Jamsie told me it's a Willie-hen."

"I know what he means," interrupted the worldlier Teke, "He means it's a cock."

"That's what it was: it must have been a cock hen," Muddle conceded.

The Doc had two long, deep-litter sheds packed to the rafters with hens of all colours and breeds. Now and again, he gave us a couple of shillings, to clear the sheds of hen-droppings. The ammonia had us high on more than one occasion.
It must have been on one of those 'highs' that Jap suggested: "'member Muddle said that, 'if you put two Willie-hens together they will fight until one of them is dead?'"
"Roosters," I corrected him.
"Cocks," Teke corrected me.
"What about them Willie-hens anyway?" I enquired.
"Well the Doc has a Rooster-hen in this shed and a Rooster-hen in that other shed…"
"Get them to have a boxing match," Teke interrupted, "Come on Gomez, we'll go and catch the other cock and bring it in here."
We caught the rooster from the other shed by throwing an old sack over him and then diving on top of him. It is a wonder he survived at all. He was not destined to survive for much longer. He was a big proud white bird. We chucked him in amongst the flock in the shed where we had

been cleaning and within seconds, the resident rooster, a massive red bird launched an attack.

Feathers flew in all directions as the rivals fought with spurs and beaks; they rose up to six feet in the air in many attacks. Eventually, the big red rooster drove his opponent off but there was nothing magnanimous in his victory – he jumped on the vanquished bird and pecked at his neck until the latter was dead.

"What are we going to do now?" moaned Teke, "the Doc had two cocks, and now he has only one."

"Could we get the dead one stuffed?" asked Jap.

"He would still be dead," I informed, "we could put him up on the rafters like he is having a wee sleep?"

"Good idea, Gomez," Jap slapped my back in appreciation of my cunning plan.

We found a ladder and propped the dead rooster in the angle of a set of rafters in the other shed. We had a great deal of trouble with his head as it kept flopping over.

"You should get his face to look like there's a happy smile on it like," Jap suggested

"But he's not very happy – he's dead," I argued.

A couple of days later the Doc arrived at our house under the pretext that he had more work for us. Although our mother protested at having to wash the clothes each time we 'dunged out' the Doc's hen-houses she gave in for she always took all the money from us. We didn't get far in the Doc's van before he muttered:

"I used to have two cocks, but now I have one," the Doc reiterated Teke's words.

"Maybe a fox got the white one," Jap suggested.

"Why would he take the white cock and not the red cock?"

"'cause the Red one could beat a fox."

"Tell me this then, young fellow: why did the fox not kill a lot of the hens as well as the cock bird?"

"'cause he got full up eating the white Willie-hen."

"Rooster," I corrected him.

"Cock," Teke corrected me.

"Cock, rooster or bloody Willie-hen: why did he hide him up on the rafters; can any one of you tell me?"

Nothing prevailed but a deadly silence – the silence of the guilty.

"Right," the Doc concluded, "You lot will clean out the other shed on half-wages."

"What did you do with the white rooster?" I asked the Doc, after a further period of silent respect.

"I left him for you lot to bury."

"In Ballycran Graveyard?" Jap enquired.

"No, I can't see Father Walsh donning his funeral robes and leading a procession, down the chapel, for a bloody dead rooster, can you?"

As I have already stated: hens played a big part in those days but not quite as big a part as they were expected to play when Flint, Teke and Jap got their hands on them. I was playing football with a boy nick-named 'Clase' when suddenly he asked me a question:

"Can hens fly?"

"A bit, not very much," I answered.

"Well there's one that has just flown down from the clouds."

"There, look, look! There's another one."

Clase was right, hens were landing amongst us from a great height and what's more: they were coming down in fairly equal intervals – a bit like Heathrow Airport in these days.

"Maybe they have escaped from an aeroplane," Clase suggested.

"I don't think so," I shook my head, for there on the battlements of Kirkistown Castle was what

looked like a pendulum with a boot on the end of it.
It was indeed: Teke's leg, swinging backwards and forwards in a definite rhythm and in between strokes, a hen was inserted into the breach by Jap, Flint or Muddle.
Then bang! A swift one up the lay-poke, swish, and another squawking hen was launched from seventy feet up into a rather uncertain future, to land amongst Clase and myself in a fluster of feathers and hen-droppings; from a great height.

My last take involving hens happened in that same Kirkistown Castle. The castle was not the tourist attraction in those days that it has become today. The place was coming down with hens. There was straw scattered everywhere to form nests in which the hens might lay their eggs. Everything had carried on for years in the same-old cycle of events; hen hatched, grows up, lays egg, family eats egg; hen lays another and so on and so on, until, that is: the fantastic four: Teke, Flint, Muddle and Jap upset the routine slightly: There was an old tradition in Ireland, around Easter time, of rolling brightly painted eggs down convenient slopes until they broke up. At that point, they were swiftly consumed, irrespective of whether they had bounced in cow-dung or not.

It was all great fun but 'once a year' was not good enough for the fantastic four; they decided to hold another Easter in July.

Muddle smuggled a rather large saucepan from his mother's house. They then gathered a quantity of yellow, gorse flowers - that which we call 'whins' in Ireland, dumped them in the saucepan, made a crude camp fire and set out for their secret mission into Kirkistown Castle and amongst Aggie Brown's hens. Gentleness was not a quality often seen in those tiny fellows, so there were a few more feathery asses kicked, a few unwelcome residents thrown out of the windows and down the stone steps until a large collection of eggs was acquired.

It was the smoke that attracted me, and I arrived as Teke, Flint, Muddle and Jap were tucking into the coloured boiled eggs.

"Why didn't you roll them down the bank?" I enquired.

"We did, but they got sand stuck to them," Teke told me.

"We've still got a whole pile left, want some?" Flint offered.

"If you all swear not to tell any of our mammies," I cautioned.

Even after taking my shared there was a dozen and a half left over.

"What we going to do with all these?" Muddle asked.

"Put them back under, Aggie Brown's hen's bums," Jap suggested.

"That's a good idea," I agreed.

"Will you help us?" asked Teke.

"No! You got them so you fetch them back.

"Will they not burn the hen's bums? asked Jap

"Cool them down in the sea, "I instructed.

"Thanks, Gomez, you think of everything," Flint was relieved.

It was never known what Aggie Brown made of matters the following morning when she went out to collect a few eggs for breakfast; only to discover that, not only were the eggs all bright yellow in colour but that they were also hard-boiled.

As a young policeman, I had a first-hand experience of an attempted electrocution. I came across a man who had wired himself to an electric socket using a pair of scissors. He had taken this drastic action just to avoid arrest, but he recovered and said that when he had thrust the scissors into the plug, he felt a massive thud, and then standing in front of him were people that he thought were dead but they were not dead and neither was he. In such cases, we hear of a sudden change in attitude for the better, but it had no such immediate effect on this small-time crook for he added the words: “So you lot can go and fuck yourselves.”

“Okay, I promise you that,” I replied, “but in return, you must promise me something,”

“And what is that then?”

“You will not try again to re-invent the electric-chair.

But back to my early case in which I realized I existed as some form of being ‘outside’ and completely independent of my body and more particularly—my brain. I am convinced these experiences led directly to the many occasions, in later life, when I stopped in my tracks abruptly and thought: ‘What the hell am I doing here?” It was as if my earthly existence was some sort of illusion or dream joke from which I would suddenly awaken. Now I look into the lost eyes of the mentally disturbed, alcoholics and drug addicts and sigh deeply when I think how ill-equipped they are to deal with life here and how many times the words have tortured their minds: “What the hell am I doing here?’

As part of my duties as a policeman I sat, night after night, guarding Albert, an old man who had been brutally assaulted and robbed of his pension book and a few coins by three creatures who thought of themselves as human beings. They had kicked Albert so hard on the head that it caused brain damage, so severe that he was unconscious and had no chance of living. Many times, on my watch, I found myself suddenly looking up from my book and silently speaking to him. I can't remember what I said or why I was urged to do it.

On the morning of the day he died, I took my leave and, as usual, silently said: "Bye Albert." I said the words silently because I was too embarrassed to let the young nurses see that I thought I could still communicate with an unconscious man.

Albert suddenly shouted, "No! No! No!" and the nurse rushed over to him and then turned and looked at me as if she required an answer from me. Sadly, I was too young and ignorant to offer any explanation.

Another old man I was delegated to guard almost caused me to take a heart attack at a very young age. I was asked to go to an address of a pensioner, who had not been seen for a couple of days.

Of course, I had a fair idea I would find him dead as that usually was the case after such reports. After breaking in, there he was; bent forward in his chair, glasses hanging off the end of his nose and with the blood drained from his face. The duty sergeant asked me to stay with the corpse until he could find his doctor to officially pronounce the old man dead. I sat down on the couch opposite the old fellow and read an out-of-date paper. I had to stop reading when it got dark as there was no money in his gas meter. Suddenly, there was a creak and the old man heaved forward and landed at my feet. I found myself in the front garden and don't remember how I got there but my heart was racing and I was gasping for breath. The window had been opened because of the smell and I still don't know whether I actually jumped out through it or went out of the door. Of course there was an explanation; rigor-mortise had taken its effect and the old man must have been sitting there just on the point of balance.

My grandmothers, on both sides were strong-minded people who had little regard for people who thought themselves important. My mother though, took after her own father who would doff his cap to anyone with two farthings to spare.

She was not afraid to stand up to 'posh' people but gave them the respect she thought they were entitled to. On day she was host to a 'Very Important Man' who was big in transport. We knew someone special was coming to our humble abode because the griddle was launched and not just for the baking of soda-bread – no, much more important – 'sods-bread with currants in it.'

The Very Important Man and his glamorous wife drew up at the front gate. He got out, inspected our gateway for size, concluded it was too small for his gleaming automobile and promptly parked it in the next-door neighbour's driveway without permission – as all very important men have a tendency to do. The driveway belonged to a man, we children referred to as: 'Daddy Adair' who lived in Belfast and simply used his Cloughey house for summer week-ends. The Targe, now on her very best behaviour, welcomed her respected guests, glancing all around to make sure that the neighbours were watching – all but Daddy Adair, that is; who was unable to see what was happening from far-off Belfast.

"More bread, Frank?" my mother enquired of the Very Important Man, "What about you, Edna?"

"Lovely, Maggie," the former answered.
"Here! Here big-fellow," as she called me in those days, for I was nearly four feet tall whilst my siblings were considerable smaller than that, "here, go and get our guests some more bread."
I returned with a very large, enamelled bread-bin which had the word: "BREAD" heavily emboss-es across it, probably so that I would not get it confused with the mop bucket. What made it unsuitable for table presentation was the bits where the enamel had chipped away were rusting through.
I plopped it in the middle of the table.

The face on my mother looked a bit like Joseph Stalin just after losing an arm-wrestling contest to Theodore Roosevelt.
"Put that bloo.. Put that thing back where it be-longs. Take out the bread and put in on a serving dish. I meant to throw that out ages ago, Edna."
"Yes, Maggie. Yes indeed," the polite lady agreed.
"What's a serving dish?" I asked.
We were quickly dispatched outside to play when the meal was finished, and that was only to save more embarrassment.

When we got outside Teke observed: "Two-thumbs can't get his wheelbarrow past our uncle's big car."

'Two-thumbs' was a nick-name, we gave to a neighbour who had an affliction of the thumbs which caused them to stick up in the air making it appear that he was continuously greeting people – a bit like John McCain in the 2006 USA presidential campaign; if you like. At that time, Two-thumbs and Daddy Adair were in fierce dispute over boundaries and access, so finding a car in his way, Two-thumbs immediately put the traffic jam down to his old adversary.

My brother ran inside: "Two-thumbs can't get his wheelbarrow past your car," he informed the important Frank.

"What size is his damned wheelbarrow," Frank growled.

"Leave it with me, I'll have a word with him," our mother went out to talk to Two-thumbs.

"Ah, ah, excuse me, William." she waved, putting on her post voice.

"Its Two-thumbs that getting blocked, Mammy," her second son corrected. He might have recognized 'Wullie' but certainly not 'William'.

When old Wullie realized that the car had nothing to do with Daddy Adair his wheelbarrow either

shrank in size or became much more manoeuvrable.
The next visit of Frank and Edna would find humour of a more subtle nature for little children had developed into young men; or a least they thought they had.

Our home, being next door to Daddy Adair's meant that we were as often on his property as we were on our own. Daddy Adair's garage was built parallel to his house and only a couple of feet separated them. This meant we could climb onto either roof using our feet and backs to edge up the walls. One day Jap was on the roof when Daddy Adair's car pulled into the driveway.
"Stay up there till they all get inside," I shouted at my little brother as the rest of us beat a hasty retreat through that garage entry and over the dyke into the top of our garden, which was called the 'Garden Grass.'
It was one of those days whereby Daddy Adair and Missus Adair took so long emptying the car boot that the daughter, Tilly, had assembled the canopied summer-seat before they had finished. This caused somewhat of a problem for a little ginger head that bobbed up and down, now and again from the rooftop. Old Willie Polly (Two Thumbs) came up from the beach with a barrow

full of white stones, saw the little ginger head, mistook it for a barn-owl or something, clapped his hands and felt proud of himself when 'the bird' disappeared. When it reappeared, he clapped his hands again and, once more, it 'flew off' and did not return because the 'bird trainer' down below was signalling it to keep down. Old Willie Polly looked at me and just scratched his head at the sight of a little boy who could communicate with birds.

"Dinner's ready," the Targe thrust her head over the half-door and shouted.
"Woops!" Here was a situation that there appeared to be no way out of: dinner was on the table and there were only two 'gannets' there to get stuck into it; the other little bird being perched up on Daddy Adair's roof.
"Dinner's bloody ready!" our mother increased the volume, "where's that other skittered japed egit?"
"Your mother is shouting for you to come and get your dinner, so you'd better come down from there," Tilly Adair shouted up to my little brother. She had been sunning and swinging herself, whilst, all the time enjoying the unfolding drama.

I have already related how my brother, Paddy, was unbeatable on his bicycle: well, one day he proved the small bike could hold its own with a car. A man called Wullie Matchett soared half-way up the Ballycran social league by purchasing himself a car – a rusty little Austin 7. Wullie not only became 'the man to be seen talking to,' but also the man to beat in a race when spotted. After church on a Sunday, my brother would wait by the side of the road until Wullie passed, or just cruise about looking for him. Either way, the object was to race him and beat him! Teke was not beaten by the Austin 7 every time, for the roads were so narrow and in such a bad state, there were places where my brother got the upper hand. One day, which proved to be almost fatal: no, not for Teke; for Wullie Matchett, the Austin 7 was spotted a hundred yards from the Quarter Crossroads. Teke was on a diagonal road and, on spying Wullie, sunk his gutties into the pedals in an effort to get to the crossroads first. The Austin 7 and 'Wullie Fangio' got there a few inches ahead of 'Patrick Merckx' but that distance was sufficiently narrow to cause a collision. One second: Teke, head down, was flying and the next; he, the little bicycle and the back door of Wullie Matchett's car were all crammed together in the

back seat of the Austin 7. The two competitors got out to examine the relative damage:
"Jesus, God Paddy!" Wullie Matchett shook his head, "You've wrecked me wee car. It looks as if you are going to have to give me a lift home on the bar of your bike."

Road traffic accidents, in my police days were a lot more serious than the event at the Quarter Crossroads. In my secondary role as Divisional Draughtsman; I was required to attend the scene of accidents involving death or likely to involve death. Some scenes I attended were absolutely horrific. A 'double-decker' bus crashed at Prescott killing a lot of passengers, mostly on the upper deck. When a crane up-righted the bus the blood flowed down the stairs. Two large lorries met at speed at Wilmere traffic lights. One was carrying tons of plastic pellets and the other lorry ended on top of that one. As we searched the scene, I examined a large mound of plastic pellets, and there I saw a white arm sticking out of it. I did not have to be told that the man on the other end would be dead. A motorcyclist was struck, head-on, on a tight bend on the Warrington Road. He was dead on our arrival but his leg was missing. I decided to search the nearby field but before I could even switch my torch on, I tramped on something soft and slippery; it was the victim's leg. With a big ex-Royal Ulster Constabulary man, I and several others attended a fatal accident in which the passengers of an overloaded car were strewn all over the place. I looked into a victim's eyes and checked his pulse for any sign of life when the big policeman came up and announced:

"Don't bother about that one Shea, he's a goner." I could tell by the shocked look in the man's eyes that he was still alive and had heard my colleague. Within seconds, the life-light disappeared from the unfortunate man's eyes and his head slumped backwards.

Not all handling of road traffic was as unpleasant as those last described but one incident led to my appearance again in front of the Chief Inspector: I noticed a long line of traffic extending down the busy Albert Road which was part of the Widnes main thoroughfare. I rode my bicycle up the pavement to pass the stationary vehicles until I reached the brow of Halton Bridge. At that point, the traffic was stationary in the opposite directions. I noticed two lorries abreast on the brow and the first thought that came into my mind was:

"Another bloody road traffic accident," and went into the centre of the road to establish where contact occurred.

What I saw were two aged drivers, with their windows wound down, and chatting away to each other. I still thought they had crashed but when I noticed them smiling and laughing, I was not so sure.

"What seems to be the matter," I got in between them.

"We're two old mates and we haven't seen each other for six years," one replied.

I simply could not believe my ears; there they were, as happy as Larry, with half a mile of traffic built up on either side of them. It was that, that prompted me to shout:

"You are two silly old buggers, and you'll not see each other for another six years if you don't get to fuck out of here – pronto!

Unfortunately, one of them must have mused over what they had done and decided to go into the police station and apologise. As the Chief Inspector sat in front of me, he read from a bit of paper he had scribbled on:

"Silly old buggers: won't see each other for another fucking six years."

"What makes you think it was me, Sir?"

"Who else? I'll tell you this Devaney; it is as well for you that he thought it was quite a joke."
"So he didn't put it in the form of a complaint?"
"Luckily for you - no, but why didn't you book them?
"A couple of miles of irate drivers, Sir."
"Get out of here."

Amongst my civilian friends, in those police days, was: 'The Wazer Morley," who initiated that friendship by offering me assistance in dealing with three or four rowdy teenagers. He, I, 'Demolition Dempsey' and 'Bashful Birch,' used to get into night-clubs, casinos and other entertainment joints on one warrant card – my warrant card. It was so bad we became referred to in the terms: "Here comes 'One warrant card and the three nods.'"
It just so happened that three complimentary tickets to the 'Matron's ball,' arrived at Widnes Police Station and the majority of policemen dared not take up the invitation for fear of how their wives might react at the prospect of their husbands wading through a room filled with willing young nurses. I wound up with the tickets and invited two of the three nodders: namely, the Wazer Morley and Demolition Dempsey to accompany me.

It was a formal-dress dance, so we had to hire out dress-suits for the occasion. To cut a long story short; none of us felt comfortable in that formal get-up, so I suggested we went somewhere appropriate to get ourselves and other used to the fact that we were dressed up as 'pretty boys.' The Wazer chose a dirty, spit-and-sawdust pub on the edge of the Mersey, much frequented by dockers and prostitutes. We sat at a grubby little table, drinking girl's drinks, using long cigarette holders and talking in posh, effeminate voices. It didn't quite work out for Demolition for he sounded like a castrated Canadian lumberjack. We certainly were the centre of attraction in that grubby little den, but it was not until I needed to go to the toilet that matters developed:

"Excuse me, Sir, but would you mind informing me as to where I could avail myself of the establishment's toiletries?" I asked a scruffy, little man who had a week's hairy growth on his pox-ridden face.

"There, here, anywhere!" he indicated, gesturing towards the saw-dusted floor.

"I thank you indeed, Sir, for your assistance, I replied, before making my way to a putrid little toilet that had a sheet of tin, hanging on a wall, to act as a mirror.

I couldn't have been in the toilet more than a few seconds when I heard someone come up behind me. A finger was stuck into my rib-cage:
"You are going to buy me a drink, aren't you?" and the finger prodded me twice or three times. I looked in the mirror, sorry, tin sheet and saw that it was none other than the dirty, little, non-shaven man from whom I had sought advice in regard to toilet facilities.
I put my hand into my breast pocket, produced my warrant card and without even disrupting the flow or bothering to turn around; flashed it (the card that is) over my shoulder and reverted to a broad Ulster accent: "This really is not your day; not only have you tapped a serving policeman but that policeman happens to come from Belfast, where this type of behaviour is quite common. I trust you have closed the door, as you came in, just to keep the noise down a bit for decapitation can be a rather rough affair if the recipient outs up any sort of resistance."

I was aware of a loud bang as if someone tried to take the door off its hinges – nothing more. When I returned to the table, I saw that Demolition and the Wazer's eyes were wide in amazement:

"What's up?" I asked.
It was Demolition that answered, in the form of a question: "Did you try to stick a tail up that little man, or something for he is off, out of the door and down the street like a bat out of hell?"
"Or something," I replied

Although all but one policemen I knew were 'straight', most of them had a fascination with what the 'benders' (as gays were known in those days) were getting up to. We often visited well known homosexual haunts such as the Long Bar in Manchester and the Magic Clock in Queen's Square, Liverpool. It wasn't policemen whom I was with the night I was put into a rather embarrassing situation by one of my mates; it was that old familiar trio, the Wazer Morley, Demolition Dempsey and Bashful Birch. It is common for ladies to accompany each other to the toilets but rather effeminate for men; except, that is: when in a bar full of homosexuals (the word 'gay' was not used in reference to sexuality as gay people in those days were thought of as well-to-do students or such out on the town). Everyone was refusing to accompany anyone to the toilet under the pretext that it might arouse suspicion. A game of outlasting each other ensued. It was a game I could not win for I was the lightest and I was drinking just as much as the others.

Eventually, I got up and went to the toilet but when I came back my mates were laughing. I knew I was in for something but wasn't sure what. A few minutes after my return, Demolition Dempsey, indicated that he wanted to whisper in my ear. As I bent forward he kissed: smack on the gob. Half an hour after the joke the Wazer Morley and Bashful Birch were still laughing. It was only when I threatened to lose my rag with them that the Wazer explained:
"It's just like this, Shea. You know the way all the fellows pinch Demolition's girls off him because he's so ugly…"
"Don't be cruel! 'Unattractive' is a better word," I interrupted.
"Well, unattractive, if you like, but it's like this: It is only a matter of time till someone tries to snatch his boyfriend off him."
"I'll bloody boyfriend you."
He was right though, because, in my absence, they had gone to a group and told them that Demolition, and I had just split up. I made up my mind that I would make a play for the next girl Demolition chatted up; even if she was the ugli-

est woman in Lancashire. As it turned out - she was.

It was in the Clockface Labour Club that became the venue for my opportunity of taking vengeance on Demolition. It had been quite a while, since the Magic Clock incident, for his chances of 'scoring' were always heavy odds against as long as there was, at least, one other man left on his feet after a night on the booze.

"Look! Look, there's your chance," the Wazer urged me, "Go on then, go on, the one he's dancing is called 'Clarissa.'

I made my way towards Demolition and Clarissa but suddenly turned back in absolute shock and a certain amount of awe.

When I reached the Wazer, I shouted at him:

"You said he was dancing with a woman!"

"He is: that's Clarissa. I told you."

"That's not a woman: that's a bloody hyena," I protested.

"Look, look! I'd be the first to admit she's not the prettiest girl on the floor but…"

"Not the prettiest!" I growled, "Her teeth are dangerous looking and those scabs all over her face reminds me of something I saw, being treated, in Manchester Zoo."

"All right! All right, I'll give you that she's a touch, just a touch, mind you like a hyena, but you do owe him one."

"Wazer, do us a favour. You already had a dose of, whatever that is, when you were in the army. The chances are that you are immune to those diseases, go on, be a pal!"

"There's a difference between being a pal and being a kamikaze pilot – fuck off!"

I had no luck that night and got the keys off the Wazer to his big, black Austin A90, got into the back seat and fell asleep. Sometime later I was disturbed by the noisy Clarissa who was moving towards the car at a hunting pace. She was being prodded on by both those big-game hunters: the Wazer and Demolition. My first thought was to find a scalable tree in which to take refuge, but I was reassured by the Wazer as he opened the car door:

"Shea, we'll drop you off first, Clarissa lives furthest away so…"

"Don't try to bluff me; you are going on Safari, both of you." I interrupted.

The following week Demolition was prowling around the same dance floor; a bit like a great, sweating bull ox on must.

"What's up with you," I enquired.

Demolition just shook his head.
"There is: there is something wrong," I insisted.
"There's nothing wrong with me, mate."
"It's Clarissa, the hyena, isn't it? You're in love!"
"Piss off!"
"Do you not want to know where she is?" I teased him.
"Not really. Well, I did think I had seen her earlier on."
"She'll be in Crombo's house by now – with the Wazer that is. You're being cuckolded mate."
"Nobody gets close enough to do that to me," he rebuked, "Not even in the Magic Clock."

I ran into my own 'Clarissa problem' in the form of a big police-woman we called 'Kirsty the Crusher.' It was better keeping a safe distance from the Crusher unless one was at the scene of a domestic dispute. Any woman giving trouble was quickly disabled by big Kirsty. For some reason, the Crusher started taking the piss out of me at every chance she got. Now-a-days, it would be classified as bullying but then it was just good fun for all in the canteen or wherever she chose to play her little game.
"Shea's so light you could chuck him from here to West Bank! If I sat on you, you'd have to be

revived. Come on Shea, let's see who can wrestle the other to the floor: ten shillings," were amongst the daily taunts.

I tried to avoid her at all costs but when that failed I tried to ignore her. Eventually, I had to give in to her challenge. I reckoned, just looking at her size, that I could physically lift her clean above my head, but the shape of her looked like it could be a problem. After a bit of an introductory tussle to gauge exactly what she had in reserve, I got a grip on a hefty leg, and the other hand got her by the scruff of the neck and I heaved the Crusher up as far as my chest but couldn't quite get her above my head. I then dropped her ingloriously, on the refreshment table. Bad, bad, bad mistake! Far from putting her off, from then on she was prowling around every corner I chanced to turn.

"I plan to have Shea's baby," she was heard to say, "Him and I could breed a little world champion," she added.

"No thanks! I don't want to be the father to a cross between a rhinoceros and a dumper truck," I responded when told about what she said.

"You do realize the Crusher just let you win that wrestling match," one policeman taunted me.

Luckily, soon after, she was transferred after grabbing some poor rowdy by the clangers in Bridge Street and trailing him into Mersey Road.

Sometimes, when I was weekend off I would go down to Bristol to see my brother and sister-in-law and of course to see their two small children. Michelle was quiet and lovely but young Stephen was quite an unbelievable child; not bad natured but up to every bit of devilment imaginable.
A neighbour came to the door: “Paddy, your Stephen has just pissed in my milk bottle.”
“How do you know it was Stephen?”
“I caught him with his little Willie in the bottle.”
“STEPHEN!”
“Yes Dad?”
“Are you pissing in milk bottles again?”
“Yes Dad.”
“Stand to attention when you are talking to me; UP STRAIGHT!”
“Yes Dad.”
“This will never happen again; DO YOU HEAR ME?”
“Yes Dad.”
“Never mind the ‘Yes Dad’, repeat after me: ‘I WILL NEVER PISS IN MILK BOTTLES AGAIN.”
“I will never piss in milk bottles again.”

"Now, if I catch you doing it again you are grounded. What will happen to you?"
"I will be grounded, Dad."

Less than fifteen minutes later my brother shouted on me to look out of the front window: "You witnessed me giving him a right bollocking just a few minutes ago; right?"
There was the bold Stephen, kneeling on top of an old Fordson Major tractor and pissing into the radiator.
"He has actually screwed the radiator cap off so that he can get pissing into the bloody tractor. Why, why, why can't he just piss into the toilet bowl like any other child?" my brother shook his head as he went to call the boy back into the house.
"We just watched you pissing into the radiator of that tractor."
The little boy stood to attention without being told: "Yes Dad."
"Not ten minutes ago, I stood you there and warned you about your pissing habits; RIGHT!"
"Yes Dad."
"But you did it again; you went straight out of the front door and did it again!"
"Yes Dad."
"Why! WHY; STEPHEN?"

"You said milk bottles, Dad."
"And you thought it would be alright to piss into a farmer's tractor – just because it happened not to be a milk bottle?"
"Yes Dad."

Mother was friendly with a farmer's wife on a farm with one cow and two pigs, one of which ate all the food and was four times the size of the other one so it might be more accurate to say 'one big pig and a quarter of a pig.' There was a cart on that farm but no horse. The horse had died, a long time before and had not been replaced. In those days mothers breast-fed their children and if size had anything to do with nourishment then the farmer's children should have been the biggest in the area. The farmer's wife took to a back room when breast-feeding the children and it was on one such feast-day that I noticed my two little brothers balancing themselves up on that bedroom window to get an eye-full of what was happening:
"Them's the biggest elders (udders) I ever seen," Teke gasped.
"Them's bigger than a cows," Jap agreed.
"Woman's elders haven't got plenty of tits on them the same as cows," Teke philosophised

“Why does she not get them milked into a bucket,” Jap enquired.
“Maybe it's because babies' mouths are not big enough to get 'round a bucket", we’ll ask Gomez.”
“No you won’t!” I thought, beating a hasty retreat around the side of the farm house for if ever there was such a thing as a recipe for going to the scene of a beating, then that was it.

It was whilst on an errand to that farm that I witnessed a gory spectacle that would remain with me for the rest of my life. Two herds of cattle grazed in adjacent fields. There must have been at least one cow ‘in season’ for a red bull (probably an Ayrshire) broke into the other field which contained a herd of Friesians and, unfortunately, a Friesian bull. Firstly, they bellowed and pawed the ground trying to intimidate each other but very soon; the smaller but more robust Ayrshire charged headlong at the taller Friesian. The latter met the red bull’s charge head-on and there was an almighty crack of horn and skull bone. It was the Friesian that was driven back. Paling-posts and barbed wire were sent hurtling through the air, and I feared that there was nothing to stop them turning on me. Although the longer horned Friesian bull badly gored the flanks of the Ayrshire bull, the smaller one did not lose one confrontation. A heavy ditch, made up of stones and sods was scattered at the monsters tumbled down the embankment unto the roadway. From there they fought their way to a raised patch of ground overlooking the Irish Sea. It was there that the brutal confrontation finally ended when the red bull drove the black-and-white bull over the rocky cliff. The victor raised his snout high and bellowed his victory call. Eventually, a neighbouring farmer controlled the Ayrshire bull by driving him off with an old Fordson tractor. I think the Frisian bull sustained such internal injuries that it had to be put down. This tremulous occurrence entered into a lot of my nightmares for the best part of my life until I actually went out of my way to pat the forehead of bulls and look into their eyes for signs of congeniality before I was released from that influence.

They say that prostitution is the oldest of all professions, but that does not necessarily mean that it should be practiced by old women as was mostly the case in Widnes where I served as a policeman. There was this old girl called Gladys Peach, who had little need to be 'on the game' as her husband was a captain at sea. I think she enjoyed the double life. If you met her when her face was clobbered in thick power and bright-red rouge she would have slobbered all over you inviting you to have a sip from her bottle of plonk as she swayed and swung it about, with the contents flying all over the place. However, if you met her when she was wearing an expensive fur coat, had just been to the beauticians and was linked in the arm of her tall husband, she would not even acknowledge you. Unfortunately, Gladys was in the former state when I got on a corporation bus with my 'best new girlfriend.' Old Peach was as 'pissed as a fart' throwing her legs up in the air exposing a fat ass that was only partly covered by knickers that were torn to pieces.

"Do you want some more of this now?" she tittered at me.

"What do you mean some MORE, you daft old bitch?"

"Aye, come on now, like you lot take advantage of a girl when you get her into that police station of yours."

"Just give me peace, Gladys."

"I'll give you something that little skinny squirt, there can't give you, have some of this," she hollered throwing the old legs in the air again.

"Just take me home safely, please," my date whimpered and so ended a beautiful friendship before it even got started.

There used to be an old saying about policemen: 'If he's not on duty, he's in the pub,' and that was true, to some extent but in my case, I usually could be found in the Vine Club, an old but cosy little building secreted away at the end of a pathway leading off Coroner's Lane, in the Black Horse district of Widnes. The Vine Club had a bar, snooker-table and a dart board and a steward called 'Chopper,' so what else could a young man need. The only commodity not supplied was girls but you could bring your own and Chopper had no objection to you staying after everyone else had gone home – provided you remembered to set the alarm and pull the door closed after you left. It was destined to be the Vine Club that would be my downfall, as far as my career in the Lancashire Constabulary was concerned. An allowance for 'police drinks' was common practice in clubs and pubs, throughout England; not just Lancashire and Chopper was certainly most generous in his interpretation of this rule.

On one particular night, I had called into the Vine Club for a couple of freebees whilst on patrol. My civilian mates were there: Bashful Birch, Wazer Morley and Demolition, with his black, horn-rimmed glasses that looked more like a pair of binoculars. The phone rang as he was lining up a shot on the snooker table. That could be something else as he used to belt the ball so hard that they had to be retrieved from all around the building, including the toilets. It was a new recruit on the phone, the man I wrote about earlier from Bolton in relation to a little accident in the cars.

"Could I speak to Shea, please?"

"Who is that?" the Wazer demanded.

"It's Bolton here, Shea give me this number, in case I felt thirsty."

"Who's Christy?"

"Thirsty, I said,"

The Wazer came to me and delivered the message.

"He'll just have to wait until I finish this game, Demolition can't keep his balls on the table," I informed my mate.

"Give me the keys and I'll go for him," the Wazer suggested.

"Good on you," I handed over the keys.

When the Wazer Morley drove up in the patrol-car, the conversation went like this, or so I am told:

"Get in," commanded the Wazer.

"Who the hell are you?" Bolton wanted to know.

"I'm the deputy, Deputy Dog if you like."

Despite his doubts, the new recruit got into the car.

"Take your helmet off! Has no one ever told you that you must take your helmet off when you're in the car?"

"Sorry!"

The Wazer and I used to frequent the nurse's home at Whiston Hospital every time I could wangle an invite to a dance or just a party, and it was on one such occasion that we chatted up these particular two young ladies.

"Has either one of you got a car?" was the question in response to the question of asking them out?

"I have," Morley responded, "now does that mean we can drop you home?"

"Is it a big car or one of those silly little Minis?"

"I'd say, it was quite a big car," I answered for the Wazer.

"It might be described as such," the Wazer agreed.

It was big indeed. It was a forty foot long coach and we were the only occupants. The Wazer has been entrusted to garage it for the night by his employers, but we had decided to take it instead of his Austin A90 – just to save on petrol.

“We’re not getting into that,” one of the girls complained.
“His dad owns it, and another fifty along with it,” I lied.
“And one day it will all be mine,” the Wazer added.
“Can I sit in the driver’s seat alongside you,” one of the girls asked my mate.

It didn’t always work out quite so well; back up in the Vine Club, on another occasion I was playing snooker, but this time with Bashful Birch and there were women involved again.
“I wish you would get a move on, Bashful, we have to get back to the ladies or they will start looking elsewhere.
“I wish you would call me ‘Basher, yes ‘Basher Birch,’ when there are young women about.
“Just take at least one shot every five minutes” I moaned.
Shortly after that we were interrupted by the Wazer Morley: “Those two Scousers are chatting up our girls.”
“Well, tell them to fuck off, I’ll be over in a minute,” I replied.
True to form, the Wazer went over to them and conveyed my message but came back almost immediately:

"They want to take me outside and beat me up."
"Accept the challenge, man. I will be with you in a couple of seconds," I had only the black ball to pot for the game.
I missed it then so did Bashful and so it went on until I was distracted by a knock on the door.
"Get that door, Shea," Chopper shouted.
I potted the black before going to the door. I opened it; there was the Wazer standing with the blood running out of his nose and mouth:
"Cheers mate!" he moaned.
"Sorry mate, forgot all about you, where are them bastards?"
"Scouseland, by now, I'd say. You owe me a fucking pint!"
"Right away! Chopper, a pint of your best bitter for my best mate here."
"Tell him to get that gob cleaned up a bit; don't want the customers thinking I'm serving raspberry juice," a sympathetic Chopper told me.

As a 'chat-up-line' I often told girls that my father was a pirate. That came easy to me for, as a child, tales of the pirates, smugglers and slave traders fascinated me. It was said that McKelvey's house in Glastery (four miles from where I was born) was built on the site of an ancient house where slaves were kept in the cellars awaiting transportation to the Caribbean and the southern states of America. Black iron rings were supposed to be sticking out of the cellar walls and the entrance to that cellar was said to be under the heavy stone that served as a front door step. We could not verify that as we were quite unable to shift the big stone, but we did try. One story though was not quite so difficult to investigate and that was: There is a smuggler's tunnel in the ancient graveyard at Slans, which is little over a mile from our old home.

The full gang set out on that special mission of investigation and amongst the tools brought on the important expedition were: two candle stumps, a lump hammer with a loose head, a shovel with a hole in it and a rusty bucket which also had holes in it but had been mended in several places using tin discs and cork gaskets, which were screwed together through the holes. Whoever was responsible for mending it, probably Muddle's father, had given up when the time came that there was more rust than sound metal left in the bucket. As we lads set out it could hardly compare to the exploration of the 'Valley of the Kings' but to us, it was equally exciting.

Once in the old graveyard, it did not take long to discover that there was indeed, what appeared to be a tunnel, the entrance of which was beneath a massive rock which I would now estimate to be twenty or thirty tons in weight. There was just enough room for small boys to force their way in. Jap was stood up on that rock on the look-out for the Watsons who owned the surrounding land and as I recall he very much resembled a meerkat with his little nose high in the air sniffing the sea breeze. The first to pop under the mighty stone was Teke, the most adventurous of us:

"Light a candle," I instructed.

"I'm trying to, but it keeps blowing out."

"Get some straw and stuff and light a wee fire," Muddle suggested.

"That's a good idea," commented the meerkat err… Jap from on top of his rocky perch.

But it wasn't such a good idea, for when Teke managed to set fire to some bits and pieces of dried grass and twigs, a belch of white smoke issued from the mouth of the tunnel and was immediately followed by a gasping, spluttering Teke.

After the fire died down Teke re-entered the gap but this time, he was followed by Flint.

"There are a whole lot of stones blocking it up," Teke shouted out of the tunnel.

"Move them then, here, get in there too, Muddle and take the bucket with you," I commanded.

After a while, I shouted in: "What's keeping you? There are three miners in there now."

"Shit!" was Teke's single word reply.

"What's up now?"

"The arse has fallen out of the bucket."

"Bloody hell! You will all just have to push the stones through to me and we will throw them in the graveyard."

"There might be blind bats in there," Jap suggested.

"Shut up!"

"Somebody has farted in here," Teke yelled out.

"Wasn't me," asserted Flint.

"Nor me," Muddle added.

"Must have been one of you couple, 'cause it wasn't me, 'cause I know the smell of my own bum," Teke yelled at his two little helpers.

After the removal of a lot more stones the stench was apparent even outside in the fresh air.

"It smells like rats in there," Jap said, pinching his little meerkat sniffer.

"Shut up! It is probably just blind bats. They do their wee shits all down the wall."

"Did you say there was blind bats down here?" Flint shrieked, emerging from the entrance.

"Blind bats can't hurt people," I tried to re-assure.

"Blind bats carry wee boys away and suck all their blood out," insisted Flint.

"What size do you think blind bats are, silly?"

"The same size as Terry duck-tails, for my daddy showed me a picture of a Terry duck-tail with a wee boy in his neb."

"Them Terry-duck…dec… things were extincted before the war started," I told Flint.

"I have found something," Teke shouted out.

"Is it treasure? I asked excitedly.

"No it's stinking," he replied.

"Is it a dead buccaneer?"

"Don't know: I have pulled a bit of his coat off him and I'll bring it out."

Teke emerged with a handful of stinking wool.

"It's a sheep! It's a stinking dead sheep," I informed the emerging miners.

"Well we can't get past it for it must be blocking the road to the pirate's treasure," Muddle sighed.

Our pride took a substantial blow one fine August day in 1946 when it was suddenly announced that we three had a little sister. It was simply unthinkable. Tough little warriors could not possibly have a sister. Such pathos was not acceptable; it would be better, just to ignore the event. She was christened 'Mary', had a little round nose, which looked like a light-bulb and when we eventually gave her the nick-name; 'Mazda' it was a sign that she was recognized – if not totally accepted. Little Mazda was lucky to survive her first years on earth and two serious matters occurred that almost took her from us. The worse was: when she was a toddler she developed double-pneumonia and scarlet fever at the same time, and it looked as if she would not make it through the night but she did for she was a little fighter.

The second time Mazda faced death resulted in an act of mercy that almost turned to tragedy. She was left in my care whilst the Targe nipped around to Molly White, who owned the local farm, for half a dozen eggs or something. I delegated my responsibilities to Teke and Jap as it was beneath a leader's dignity to look after a little girl. I went up the garden to play but, during that time, little Mazda started to cry. Now, if a baby cried, according to the psychology of Teke: she must be hungry.

"I'll get the gully-knife out and cut some bread and you can feed her," he instructed young Jap. Cutting big lumps of bread off a loaf and feeding them to a six-months old child may not be recommended as a healthy diet but one thing it does do; it certainly stops them crying. When our mother returned the child's little face was so stuffed with bread that she looked like one of those big-headed gudgeon we used to catch off Charlie's Rocks. It goes without saying that; after the child was rescued there ensued a period of dangling Tammany Nominees and red-raw little butts.

In the mid nineteen sixties Lancashire County Council eventually granted the police in Widnes enough cash to build themselves a new police station. It was much bigger than the old place and therefore needed a lot more personnel to fill it. When you bring in more beat-bobbies, you have to employ more people to supervise them and that was the reason we got a new batch of sergeants with a couple of inspectors thrown in for good measure. Amongst the sergeants was one: Jack Leatherballs who soon got down to the business of the two 'B's' – booze and blackmail. In those days, there was always a certain low level of corruption; involving such professions as;

licensed premises, ice-cream vans, bookmakers and garages:

- A blind eye was turned to licensees doing 'a spot' after hours as long as the neighbours didn't complain of the noise or the ring of the till could not be heard from the street.
- Ice-cream vans were selling fags and stuff to the occupants of high-rise flats and whilst we turned a blind eye to local vendors, those from outside the town were threatened with searches.
- Many small bookmakers were operating without a permit or license for their premises but were generally left alone as long as they did not draw too much attention to themselves by welshing on bets or something similar.
- Damaged cars were toed in by garages favoured by whichever cop got lumbered in reporting the accident.

In general, recognition of one's services usually was a round or two of drinks when officers met up with those who benefited through their discretions. Mostly, the meetings could be described as 'chance encounters' but on other occasions, they might not have been quite by accident, ac-

cording to how close pay-day was. Sergeant Leatherballs was something else though; in uniform or out of it, he demanded his drinks from pubs and clubs, never paid for his bets with the bookmakers and set a minimum price for garage toe-ins. I do not know what his special tariff was on ice-cream vendors, but the Foran brothers used to switch off their jingles and beat a hasty retreat when they saw him approaching. Leatherballs was seldom sober whilst on duty and Trevor Blenn, a colleague, and fellow countryman, of mine, whispered in my ear at the scene of a crash caused by a drunken driver:
"We would have a stronger case if we could get Leatherballs to piss in the bottle."

A gem of an incident happened just off the M6 motorway and is worth mentioning here although I was not involved in it:
A driver was feeling a bit peckish, spied a 'chip-van' just after he turned off the motorway and pulled in behind it. Unfortunately, it appeared that the shutters were closed and the people inside were preparing to leave the scene and go home.
"Come on! Come on!" the irate driver battered the side of the van, "I need a fucking chip, open the fucking hatch, there."

The occupants did: they were two policemen, and the van was a breathalyser unit parked on the grass verge.

"What can we do for you, Sir?"

"I only wanted a chi.. chip, sorry?"

"Sorry we don't do chips but I'm sure you won't mind blowing into this here, Sir," one of the officers stuck a tube into his gob.

The driver, who was registered nearly twice the legal limit was fined a hundred pounds and banned from driving for two years.

The Wazer Morley was an auxiliary fireman and often he would dash off in the middle of a sentence if his house-bell sounded to indicate a report of a fire somewhere. He was a good fireman if not somewhat of a rash one. A day in which I had arrived first at a fire in a shed in an ICI complex, the Wazer arrived on his gleaming fire tender; he was armed to the teeth, with blood-red axe, long studded boots, tin snips and hacksaw at the ready and was soon doing lead man on a big powerful hose.

"This way men! Follow me," he hollered glancing at me to make sure I witnessed just how important he was.

He kicked open a wooden door, where white fumes were leaking from the jambs, switched on a powerful jet of water, dashed in, head first and within a second there was a great explosion and there was the Wazer, flying back out of the door again and away above my head and gallantly still holding unto his trusty hose. Actually, I think they call it a 'branch' but it looked more like a hose to me.

"That's rather spectacular; even for the Wazer," I thought, "I wonder has he set this up for my benefit?"

"He's just gone and blasted water unto a sulphur fire, hasn't he," the voice, from behind me, sounded familiar.

It was our mate Demolition, who worked in the ICI at the time, and he though the whole incident was simply hilarious: "He has really done it this time, hasn't he," Demolition laughed, "This is even worse than the time he spewed up over the nun on the ferry to Birkenhead."

"No, he's not much of a sailor," I agreed.

"Not much of a fireman either, if you ask me."

"He would make a good human-cannonball," I ventured.

"He would" at last Demo and I, were in agreement about something.

Although Demolition and the Wazer were really good friends, working for the same firms for

most of their days, they were forever playing pranks on each other. One example is: Demolition packed lorries in the same place that the Wazer Morley was supposed to be operating a 'knife machine'. Morley hated the knives and used to clock in late so that someone else was deputised to take his place. After clocking in he wouldn't even inform anyone he had actually turned in for work and spend most of the shift torturing Demo. He told me he would make Demolition Dempsey world famous:
"Without mentioning the hyena," I enquired.
"Without mentioning the hyena," he assured.
He went on to disclose how he used a can of black spray to draw a gigantic pair of glasses, signed 'D' on the side of every container Demolition was involved in packing. As I have already pointed out; Brian Demolition Dempsey wore heavy horned-rimmed spectacles. I often saw such containers pass by when I was on patrol. I thought nothing much of that, but some twenty-five years later, when a container bearing that 'logo' passed me in Ireland, memories flooded back.

All three: Demolition Dempsey, Bashful Birch and the Wazer Morley applied, at various times, to become drivers of Widnes Corporation busses.

Demolition smoked a packet of Capstan Full Strength cigarettes each day and was turned down on the grounds that his recovery time took too long; an hour every morning; spluttering over the sink. Bashful lost out on the fact that he spent ten minutes checking that the gear-stick, handbrake and other controls were in the same place as they had been when he was first introduced to the bus. Only the Wazer got a job but the superintendent was to regret his decision as my mate turned out to be rather unconventional. For example: when he was on the Cronton Colliery run and in the queue of busses awaiting the miners, when it came his turn, he would suddenly close the doors and drive off, still empty, with a stampede of the underground workers battering the sides of his bus. At other times, he would stand at the door inspecting miners for the slightest trace of coal-dust.

"You're not coming unto my bus covered in fucking soot," he would shout, pushing selected miners to the side. I say 'selected' for he made sure not to pick on those who would kick his shins to pieces.

When he was reported for driving off with an empty bus, he argued that his vehicle was packed and asked the superintendent was he going to take his word or the word of a pack of 'moles' who had spent all day in the darkness and whose eyes and not acclimatized to the light on the surface. The superintendent took the word of the 'blind moles' and the Wazer Morley was sacked.

The part of Ireland where I was born is renowned for fervent, religious views and very little charity towards those who oppose such views. The village of Cloughey had its share of religious zealots, and most Sundays would see a congregation of open-air preachers endeavouring to win souls for Jesus Christ – as if he hadn't enough trouble with the ones he already had. Pastor Eddie Graham led the Cloughey and Kirkistown preachers. For a megaphone, he used a tin, milk jug which had the ass knocked out of it. My mother gathered with her friends in our garden to listen to 'testaments' of those who maintained they had seen the light, for there was precious little entertainment in the forties, outside the radio, which was very much dependent on someone having remembered to have the battery charged up in Mister Keene's shed.
Eddie Graham was the first man to come out with the statement: "You are like a boat with a hole in the bottom; the first test of your faith and you sink to the bottom of the sea. Thank God there is no hole in my bottom."

"You'll be needing a right dose of castor-oil, if you ever get 'round to having a hole bored in your arse," Lilly Gibson shouted over at him. Flint's question had everyone laughing for when the pastor announced, for the umpteenth time, that he had 'seen the light' the little boy asked his mother: "Mammy, did Mister Keene put new electric sparks in his house too?"

Flint lived with his mother away beyond the end of the 'Warren' (our play-heaven) and almost right down on the shore. Beside them lived a very old lady by the name of Minnie Quinn. Her house was so old: it was from before the days when it was thought necessary to lay a solid floor. In other words: her home had earthen floors; the very ground on which it was first built. Constant sweeping over hundreds of years had put a shine on the earth and it was quite nice to look at – apart from the odd bumpy patch here and there. One day we could see black smoke on the sky-line but the problem was: the smoke was inter-laced with tongues of bright red flame.

"That's Minnie Quinn's house on fire!" I shouted.

"What we going to do?" asked Flint.

"We have to get some sea and put it out," suggested Teke.

“Minnie Quinn will be burnt like a witch,” Muddle said.
“We have to tell Mister Keene to get the fire-brigade,” I decided.
“Good idea, Gomez,” Jap agreed.
“I’ll go and get Daddy’s bucket,” Muddle offered.
“Good idea, Muddle,” Jap again agreed.

Frederick Keene must have seen us running towards his little shop for he met us on the doorstep:
“Now, what has happened, boys?”
“Minnie Quinn’s house is on fire; you have to come quick. You have to get the fire-brigade,” I panted.
“Minnie Quinn is been burnt like a witch,” Flint told him, “and she’s got chickens to look after,” he added as an afterthought.
“Calm down, calm down, boys,” Mister Keene reassured us, “It is only a chimney fire; she must have been burning papers or something and the soot in her chimney has caught fire.”
Mother later disclosed that, as usual Fred Keene missed nothing and had Minnie Quinn’s house under his ‘telescopic’ gaze right from the fire starting.

After we had been talking to him for a few moments, Muddle returned with his father's bucket. You would not believe it, but it had a hole in it as well.

"What were you going to do with that bucket?" Mister Keene demanded an answer.

"We were going to put the big fire out with the sea."

"Put it out with sea water! There's a damned hole in that thing. Every time you got the bucket back to the house it would be empty," Mister Keene made little allowances for children's logic. I wonder did the bloody man think that after bringing the bucket back once and finding it empty would we go on repeating the trip down to the sea and back with the water pissing out of the bucket?

I have mentioned that the Wazer Morley was an auxiliary firemen, well, it just so happened that auxiliaries were not exactly 'flavour of the month' with the regulars at Widnes Fire Station. One night when the Wazer was driving me home from the Vine Club we heard the fire engine. Morley chased it with a view to claiming his 'turn-out' fee. This did not go down well with a particular regular fireman who decided to frame both him and me for making a malicious call as the fire phone-call turned out to be a hoax. We were both interviewed by the Widnes CID but of course we knew simply nothing about the call. I found out who had instigated the complaint and bided my time. Some six months later the fire-brigade was taking part in an annual charity event with the offending 'fire-bobby' driving the engine. He stopped it on double yellow lines. As it was not an emergency, I booked him. I could tell by the look on his face he knew what was behind it.

I am told that the Chief Superintendent hit the roof, shouting: "What the hell is that man playing at – Lancashire Council versus Lancashire County Council."

Sergeant Leatherballs grinned at me: "What took you so long?"

The writing was on the wall for my police career when Demolition Dempsey decided to throw a party at his home in Deacon Road. Norman Scott and I were invited.

"What's it in aid off," I asked Demo.

"It is the anniversary of the day the Wazer spewed over the nun in that epic crossing of the Mersey," he replied.

"Fair enough, that will do us fine," I accepted.

"We're on nights on that date," Scott reminded me.

"And when did that stop you going to a party?" Demolition exclaimed.

"Okay, okay, we'll be there, but we might have to nip out now and again for it's a Saturday night"

"What do you and Scott do on a Saturday night, throw stones at the drunks leaving Simmies?"

He did not realize how close he was to the truth – on that night, at any rate.

We spent the best part of the night at Demolition's party, booked off at six in the morning, returned to it and started heading home a little before seven. Just our luck: as we got into Albert Road, two drunks who had just been thrown out of the Regency club picked a fight with us. They didn't win; as a matter of fact, both found themselves in someone's front garden having been unceremoniously, turfed over the hedge. An argument ensued as to who had disposed of their opponent the quickest. This resulted in a challenge to see, which could put the other over the next hedge. As this drunken, full uniformed, contest was heating up some 'spoilsport' decided to report the matter to the police station. In their wisdom, the office staff sent a young recruit to deal with the disturbance. No prizes for guessing where he wound up – in someone's front garden. In no time, the street was full of police cars, even motorway patrol cars. There was a stand-off for most realized that the task was not going to be an easy one. It was left to the wonderful little Sergeant Twitch, who instructed those present that the best way to deal with two Gallic renegades was to talk quietly to them. Night after night, day after day we awaited the outcome. Nothing happened, which reminded me of that instructor telling me it was harder to get thrown out of the force than to stay in it. However, I still managed it. I later made amends with the young recruit we had thrown over the hedge by introducing him to the girl he was to marry, who turned out to be one wonderful lady and mother and remains a friend of mine till this very day.

Teke may not have been at the top of the academic tree but 'streetwise' he left us all a long way behind. You may think that the philosopher's stone was a load of old hogwash, but I can tell you, Teke was into its equivalent when he was no age. Young Jap and I used to feel envious of our brother who always appeared to dine better than we did; leaving a trail of multi-coloured, sweet papers behind him as he went hustling the tourists across the Warren. Certain bottles carried a redemption value of three pence, but he would never accept a threepenny-bit – it always had to be three big copper pennies. It all unfolded the day Big Bessie chased him across the 'sinky sand' firing a saucepan at his little sandy head, stopping to retrieve it before it disappeared in the sludge, gather speed once more, take aim again and release the missile another time.

"Save me! Save me, Gomez. Big Bessie thinks I'm giving her pennies," he yelled at me.

"Does Big Bessie not like pennies anymore," I enquired, quite innocently.

"Not when they are supposed to be bloody half-crowns," Big Bessie hollered back at me.

What had happened was: Teke had got his hands on a bottle of tin-chloride, which was supposed to be for repairing mirrors and had been silvering pennies with it and passing them off as half-crowns. He usually bought only one 'penny gob-stopper' with Big Bessie and spent the change with Mister Keene. He was wise enough to know that Mister Keene would never have fallen for his scam.

I had a friend at school, affectionately known as 'Micky Doe' who kept me well informed of plots to overthrow me as leader of the school-kids.

Some of the plots were real and some were invented by Micky Doe as he saw himself as Ballycranbeg Public Elementary School's answer to the renowned boxing promoter Harry Levine. One day he whispered in my ear:

"The two Bimbo's are going to hijack your brother and knock the shit out of him."

"When, Micky?"

"Home time."

"Where, Mickey?"

"The chestnut tree."

I made sure I was out of the school-yard like a bat out of hell and into the lower branches of the chestnut tree before anyone, except Micky Doe, had rounded the corner. The two Bimbos were not long behind me and took up a position below me. Teke emerged from the school lane.

"We have got something to sell you," the bigger Bimbo shouted over at my brother.

"What is it?"

"Come here and see."

Teke made his way towards them, but he was cautious. I took the opportunity to jump out of the chestnut tree right unto the shoulders of the bigger Bimbo, knocking him to the ground, which is not surprising; it was sheer luck that I did not kill him. The season's last remaining chestnuts dropped on the prostrate lad as if to signal a hollow victory. Teke caught on immediately and launched into the smaller Bimbo. The two Bimbos scrambled to their feet and were off, so ending what was to be the first of many attempted coups.

"I was here in case you needed back-up," Micky Doe assured.

In Widnes, it was seldom that the Vine Club saw itself catering for anyone of any importance, yet, once a year they hosted the annual dinner dance for the directors of that division of ICI. It was a formal occasion with the town dignitary being guests of honour.

Chopper Morris gave us our annual instructions:

"Remember lads keep clear of here tomorrow night. It is the annual dinner dance and we will have important people about."

"Chopper's getting a bit above his station," the Wazer whispered to me, "I mean, who does he think he is, barring us from his own club?"

"Meet me here at eight o'clock," I instructed, "and Wazer..."

"What?"

"Bring that daft silk house coat you have at home; you know the one that looks like a Buddha monk's kaftan or whatever they wear."

At eight o'clock, the following evening, the dinner was progressing as planned in the newly decorated Vine Club. Presentations were in full swing as we peeped around the door. A catering company was hired to provide the victuals; a professional master of ceremonies was present and Chopper was reduced to the roll of keeping out undesirables, although he too was in evening dress or perhaps a dinner suit for I can never tell the difference. I was dressed in the red silk house coat, and the Wazer had pulled a car rug over his shoulders. I had a dirty old wine bottle in my hands and in it was the biggest nettle you ever saw. The Wazer carried a house brick. Chopper Morris tried to prevent us entering but I flashed my warrant and cautioned: “Official business, step aside please.” He was taken aback long enough to allow us through.

We entered the dining area and slowly walked between the two long tables, bowing deeply, every so often humming that ‘ohm’ thing like the Buddha monks do. I think the Wazer farted in the middle of it for he was good at that; he could pass wind almost at will. He always maintained if he found himself in the presence of certain people it gave him the urge. We approached the little stage where the master of ceremonies was presenting the annual awards and knelt down in front of him in reverence. We then slowly arose and I presented to him the dirty wine bottle with the big nettle sticking out of it.

"What is it?" he stuttered.

"Why, it's a nettle, my good man," I replied.

"But why?"

"It is a sign of irritation, the nettle, Sir. And the dock-leaf takes away the great stinging itch and therefore, is a sign of peace."

"But we couldn't find a dock-leaf in the dark, Sir so we brought along this brick. I trust you will receive it with the good-will that was intended, Sir?"

"I think there must be some sort of mistake, my good men," the official protested.

With that Chopper appeared. His growling face had taken on a smile of extraordinary proportions, and he was clapping his hands vigorously:

"Thank you very much, thank you very much, gentlemen. We thought we would give you a little light entertainment as a surprise," he turned to the diners and continued his clapping. The guests quickly adopted the spirit of the occasion and broke into rapturous applause.

Chopper ushered us away and into the snooker room: "If you two do anything like that again, your freebees are fucked for life. Now sit down there and shut up and I will pull you a couple of drinks. Then you must leave; understand?"

"Yes, Chop."

I already mentioned that there was a farm at the top of our garden and it was owned by Molly White. Well, Molly White had three nanny-goats and these nanny-goats provided the five of us with hours of fun; the kind of fun that would get you locked up now-a-days for cruelty to animals. Goats are notoriously hard to keep fenced in so Molly White tethered her three nanny-goats on long ropes in the field used for grazing. It was easy to tell the length of the tethers by looking at the circle of short grass each goat had shorn. This knowledge acted as the safety device in the game we called 'the nanny-goat run.' The rules were simple.

- One point won, if you entered the circle, shouted: "Nanny-goat, nanny-goat, nanny-goat run" and managed to get out of the circle again.
- Three points if you got close enough to kick the nanny-goat up the ass and get away with it.
- Two points: both them up your own ass if the nanny-goat caught you.

Invariably, we got back out of the circle without harm only for the poor nanny-goat to come to a jolting halt when it literally came to its tether's end. One day things went horribly wrong when Jap entered the circle of the little nanny-goat without noticing that she had slipped her tether. "Nanny-goat, nanny-goat, nanny-goat run," and he was swiftly off to the edge of the circle. It was when my little brother turned that he saw she had no tether on and was coming full blast in his direction. But she reckoned without taking into consideration the nimble feet of little Jap. He side-stepped the small nanny-goat; with the dexterity of a seasoned Spanish bull-fighter, and left her charging headlong into her neighbour's territory. The big nanny-goat duly drove her off and we pulled Jap back over the hedge to safety.

One day our mother called us together and announced that Father and she had decided to move to one of the new houses that Henry Gilmore had built on the Castle Grounds. I was simply thunderstruck. I could not believe I would not walk all those familiar little paths again; never again sit in my saddle-back tree, jump off the old burn structure into a raging sea nor catch fish on Charlie's Rocks. She said she had sold the old homestead but that the purchaser wished not to

be named at the present but said that we would know in good time. When the day came for us to depart, I seemed to be the only one who was sad. I walked my little paths for the very last time, scratched my initial on the old burn structure, hugged the saddle-back tree and then sobbed my heart out. Mother handed over the keys to: Mister Keene.
My childhood days were over.

On the outskirts of Widnes, there was (and still is) a fine little pub called 'The Four-topped Oak.' Sergeant Jack Leatherballs had a habit of landing into the Four-topped Oak just before his refreshment period and raiding the big fridge of several meat pies and then disappearing without paying. It was that pub that Hughie Mitchel decided to hold his promotion party in. It was an all police affairs, so I had to think up a very cunning plan to gain the Wazer admission. We dressed up as two old tramps, rubbing dirt into our faces and hands, collecting two grubby tins of cigarette ends and dressing in early twentieth-century clothes that Morley's father had hanging in his shed. Two old felt hats pulled down in such a way that our ears were sticking out, together with thick horned-rimmed glasses perched on the ends of our noses, totally set the scene. The one person who had to be in on the act was: the landlord or we would have been ejected for sure.

We bought a half-pint of mild beer and shared it between us before filling the glasses up with water and lighting up several buts and all the time we kept mumbling, head nodding and faking senile shakes. The party couldn't really get swinging for everyone was focused on us old tramps. Several wanted to ask us to leave but big-hearted Hughie would not let them saying: "They are doing nobody any harm, just let them be." The Wazer had cut the ass out of the ancient pair of trousers he was wearing and when he opened the big safety-pin a patch of about two square feet fell onto the floor.

Kirsty the Crusher and her friend began cat-calling: "That's not a bad shaped arse for an old tramp," the former yelled out.

"Why don't you go over and give the Crusher a kiss," Morley suggested.

"Fuck off! Why don't you?"

He did but she pretended she didn't like it.

I pinned the patch back on him for it could have been a give-away. Of course, the Wazer pretended I was sticking the pin into him but his yelps of supposed pain only caused a lot more laughter.

Even when we tried to gate-crash the buffet room, Hughie Mitchel was magnanimous:
"Sorry, Pops, this is a bit of a private party, but if you go back out into the bar I'll bring you both a couple of sandwiches."
"I don't like cheese, Hughie," I spoke in my natural voice.
"Hey you bastard," he slapped me on the back; "you know what? I was a bit suspicious for tramps should stink you know."
"I tried my best but I couldn't bring one on, sorry," the Wazer apologised.

In the old Vine Club, Chopper had forgiven us our misdemeanour with the nettle and brick, and on the particular night, the drinks were flowing freely and everyone was making merry. I should have sensed that something was not quite as it should have been; there was no sign of Sergeant Jack Leatherballs, his mate, Des Balmy or, for that matter, any of the beat constables appearing for their nightly freebees. It was about one o'clock in the morning when suddenly there was loud banging on the back door:
"Police! Open up, police"
"It's a raid! It's a bloody raid!" I yelled at those still drinking.

The customer thought I was up to one of my old tricks again and burst out in laughter. As a player and I pushed the heavy snooker table up against the rear door, I shouted: “Man the other doors, keep them out! Throw the bloody drink away. Chopper responded and went to defend the front doors, but the other just rolled about laughing and shouting such things as:

“Hilarious, hilarious, Shea! Where do you get them from?”

I went to give Chopper a hand and managed to push one of my mates back out of a window that had been breached. Suddenly, the place was swarming with uniformed police and still the customers drunk merrily.

“Everyone stand by your own drink,” Sergeant Des Balmy shouted out.

He then came over to me and whispered: “Of course, Shea, you were our man on the inside.”

I just shook my head and replied: “I have done many things I am not proud of, but I will not step that low.”

I was fined one pound at Widnes Magistrates’ Court but I would not pay it on principle. My good friend Sergeant Norman Potts payed it without my knowledge (when, thirty years later I went to visit him as he lay on his death-bed he

smiled and uttered: “It must be the end of the world; “Shea has returned.” How ironic!)
My police days were over.

The most important mission of all, on acquiring the new house, was a special invite to some people of substance and those people happened to be the wealthy relatives; Frank and Edna whom I introduced earlier. Father, who was at home on the day of the VIP’s next visit, had bought a second-hand Grundig tape recorder and taught me how to operate it. When everyone was seated at the table for tea, the tape-recorder was switched on and the stage was set for my first venture into satire.

“It was just when we were about to clench the deal that tragedy struck…” the Very Important Man held us all in awe.
When I later edited the tape it went like this:
The VIP: “It was just when we were about to clench the deal that tragedy struck.
Superimposed: “the MD took short.”
The added sound effect was a simulated fart followed by the flushing of our new water-closet, of which we were very proud if I may add.
Another one was:

The VIP: “It would have been around the time that the good Queen Mother died, Mary of Tech as she was formally known.”
The sound effects added to that one were a scream: “Ayeeeeeeeeeeeeeeeee!” followed by the bursting of a balloon.
Another thing I remember the VIP saying was:
“It was then that I spied an opening, a niche in the market, if you like…”
When later doctored this became: “It was then that I spied an opening and made my escape only for the warders to send the blood-hounds after me.”
And so Frank provided a mass of material that I manipulated after his departure. My mother wanted nothing to do with the doctored tape, but my father played that old tape so many times and still asked about it, many years later, when I was in the Lancashire Constabulary.
“You should have kept that, you know. Somebody might have bought it someday; that is the way humour is going to be in the future,” he once said.

The year was 1954. Two youths were cycling home when they were confronted by an awesome sight. It was near midnight on a dark clouded winter's night when suddenly the sky ahead lit up by a fire of great intensity. Although the blaze was obscured by the hill, the heavy clouds pulsating orange, red and black left the youths in no doubt as to what lay ahead.

"God that's some fire!" stuttered the eldest of the youths.

"It's the end of the world," gasped the other.

They were unable to see the source of the fire until clear of the surrounding low hills and adjacent with the old aerodrome. The sight that met their eyes was terrifying; a building, some three stories high, ablaze in the night sky.

The burning timbers were breaking loose and falling into the basement, throwing blazing fragments and sparks out of the lower windows. Most of the roof had gone and flames soared twenty to thirty feet into the dark sky, causing the clouds to shimmer and dance in the violent colours of fire. Dense black smoke drifted towards the youths. There was something very strange about that inferno; there was no sound - no roaring, crackling, or explosions. The fire was consuming the building with the silence of death. The younger youth was my school pal, Colm Gilmore and the elder youth was I.

My pal’s face glowed in the reflected light and in his eyes I saw fear - fear of the unknown. We stood in silence for a minute or more, balanced between astonishment and a compelling urge to run. Something inside pushed me forward. I began to climb the big wooden gate that separated us from the aerodrome but stopped when I realized there was no heat in the air and that there shouldn't even have been a building there in any case. I turned back to tell my friend but everywhere was suddenly pitch black - I could not even make out where he stood.

He spoke: “It's gone!”

I looked back into the aerodrome. Nothing but a black, eerie silence remained.

Could it have been a dream? Could two people dream the same dream at the same time? Could we have been dreaming when we were not asleep? I now know the answer, but it has taken me a lifetime to find it out. It is down to that ‘old devil’ again—time, but I shall let you into the secret towards the end of this story.

When the three elder boys went to secondary school the names, Gomez, Teke and Jap faded, but I shall continue to use them so not as to confuse the reader – should there be any unpaid ones. In secondary education, my form master was a little man, in his late twenties, called Lennox. The lack of height of this teacher was to be the undoing of many who 'took him on.' In my brother, Teke's case it was altogether more sinister. He was ascending the stairs in Newtownards Technical School when he espied, his good friend; Roy Halliday and summarily grabbed him by the stones. A little face turned, and the little face was angry and the little face belonged to 'Mister Lennox:' as a matter of fact, the stones belonged to Mister Lennox He didn't ask for an explanation but simply smacked Teke one under the chin tumbling his to the bottom stair. It was a good two minutes before my brother regained the same position on the stairwell as he had occupied prior to the mishandling of another man's private property. Now the moral of this story is: if you are intent on grabbing someone by the gools – check out as to whom they are hung on before taking action.

It took Teke some weeks at the new school before he thought up a scam that would keep him up to the standard of living to which he has become accustomed. He invented a little gadget that could be inserted into a chewing-gum machine in place of a penny, but the trick was: it could be retrieved and used in multiple occasions and was only abandoned when police or teachers were spotted in the vicinity. He was reselling his ill-gotten goods at three for tuppence. The legitimate traders simply could not compete, most especially because they were expected to re-stock the machines, although I don't believe there was any written contract, to that effect. The scam came to an end when one of the chewing machines went haywire spitting out chewing-gum balls like a Thompson's sub-machine gun. Hundreds of those tiny, coloured balls trundled their way down South Street and at the head of them was one: Teke, running like the clappers whilst, with one hand, holding his school-cap in place and with the other, placed on his little fat ass in case the shop-keeper caught up with him.

One of the Tech teachers was called Bouncer Brown. Bouncer's favourite pastime was requesting pupils to place their hands on a desk, whilst he beat their knuckles with the edge of a ruler. An even more favoured pastime of his was: doing it to my brother.

"When I'm a big man I'm going to come back and give you a dig in the teeth," Teke threatened him.

"Paddy, if I have heard that once I have heard it a hundred times and do you know how many have been able to carry out that threat: precisely none!"

"I'll be the first then," my brother promised.

A few years later Teke met Bouncer Brown in the hallway of Wallace's chemists in Newtownards:

"Do you remember me?" Teke asked him.

"No. Why, should I?"

"Perhaps this will help your memory," said my brother and smacked him one on the gob which laid the Bouncer Brown out flat in the porch way of the chemists.

My vengeance on the bully Cesspit, was not quite so dramatic. I grew considerably bigger than he did. As a matter of fact, he didn't grow much more at all since his school days:

"Remember you used to bully my little brothers and me when we were caddying at the golf club?" I confronted him.

"What of it?"

"Well, I'm going to bully you now but only for as long as you manage to stay on your feet."

We went outside, and I put on a pair of leather gloves.

"You can't wear them; that's an advantage," Cesspit protested.

"Just you hold on there, and I will borrow a pair for you," and I left him to do so.

When I came back Cesspit was heading off:
"Where are you off to, I thought you were going to fight me," I shouted after him.
"I forgot, I haven't had my tea yet," he yelled.
"Don't forget to come back now, after your tea that is. Remember I have got a present for you."
I never saw Cesspit again in my lifetime.

Before our family were, 'signed, sealed and delivered' we had two more sisters and one more brother and, of course, they all got pet names. The eldest of the last trio was 'Wee Wong'. No she had nothing to do with the People's Republic of China but got that nick-name through her elder sister (Mazda) not being able to pronounce; 'Yvonne' and the day little Yvonne, as a toddler, recited to the chiming of the old clock:
"Wee Wong, ding dong,
"Ding dong, Wee Wong."
My God, she had a tremendous spirit. We three older lads used to jump twenty feet into the pit that was excavated behind our new house, but if you didn't catch and dislodge the shale half way down you could wind up with a broken leg. One; me' two; Teke, Three; Jap all landed safely. It was a bit like counting in planes returning to their parent aircraft carrier. Four; - what do you mean – four? Good God it was out little sister,

Wee Wong', holding her skirt in the up-draught like a parachute and coming in to land. She did it perfectly. If only we had known, then that she would never grow old.

The youngest boy became 'Texas Sam' and that name was well-earned, for from morning until night, he was a little cowboy. When the rest of his mates had their fill with gun-slinging and arrow shooting, he would often ask us older ones to play cowboys and Indians with him.

"Who is to be the Indian," I asked, as if I didn't know.

"You can be the Indian; I'll be Texas Sam."

"But the Indians never win, do they?"

"Sometimes they do, 'cause Indians are good at hiding you know," he tried to convince me.

No harm to Texas Sam, but I did not find that to be true; neither in real life nor in his little games. No matter how well I thought I had concealed myself, I would feel 'cold steel' pressed into my ribs accompanied by that famed command:

"Hands up."

On one occasion, I had hidden in a big, old, rusty oil-drum and was tittering away to myself at the fact that I had been there, undetected, for quite a while, when suddenly a gun was pressed into my ass, accompanied by the words: "Hands up."

He had his little gun poked through the hole where a distribution tap had once been. I swear to God that, that wee lad must have been born with heat-sensors attached.

Like her eldest sister, the youngest girl was born with a little round nose and consequently got the pet name 'Neta Bulb' for it was that bit smaller than Mazda's. This didn't last long for soon she was referred to as: 'The Wane,' which is simply another name for 'baby' in our neck of the woods. Now that did stick for when she was in her late fifties she made a special request that it be terminated:

"When you call me 'The Wane' people look at me, and I know they are thinking: 'Now there's no harm, for a woman, in taking a few years of her age, but that is pushing it a bit,'" the Wane protested.

The Wane was the Targe's eyes and ears. Not only was she the fly on the wall, the spy in the camp, but she was so thorough at her job, she could anticipate just what you would get up to next and seldom was she wrong. Texas Sam was the victim in most cases but he fought back; he would discretely point a little finger at the Wane and keep it there until her nerve gave way and she complained to our mother. Ninety per-cent of the time Texas Sam wound up with cuffed lugs but for some reason, best known to wild westerners, he thought it was well worth the suffering. He was absolutely brilliant at his chosen torment. He could pick his nose, poke his ear, scratch his head and always leave a rigid finger pointing in the direction of the Wane. One particular occasion I remember well was: Texas Sam was scratching his bum, as all good cowboys do from time to time, when a protest rang out loud and clear:

"Mammy, he's pointing at me again."

"I'm scratching my ass."

The Targe lowered the eyebrows: "I've been watching you, my lad, and unless you withdraw that bloody finger of yours, I'll ram it right up your skinny little arse, accompanied by the toes of my boot."

A couple of minutes later: "He's doing it again, Mammy."

"What the hell is he at now?"

"He's pretending to scratch his Tammany Nominee."

There was a loud crack that echoed around the four walls and it was the Wane that held her face for a change.

"Don't you ever let me hear you use that word again! Tammany Nominees are boys' affairs and

have nothing to do with girls and never will if I have anything to do with it."
A bit naive, if you ask me.

Our mother did not like to be proven wrong nor did she like to be embarrassed as had happened in the taxi without brakes fiasco but that was mild compared to what occurred one day in Ballycran Church. In those days, the collection plate consisted of a wooden box on the end of a long pole. It was probably to enable the collector to keep an eye on who put what into it. The Doc was that official in Mount St Joseph. A fair amount to put into the collection box would have been a threepenny bit but most were pennies with the odd halfpenny thrown in usually accompanied by either a red face or a strong smell of drink. On the day in question, Mother needed a penny change from her threepenny bit, so she might have enough to pay for the Sunday papers, so she tossed in the little brass coin and fingered around in the box for a penny. Unfortunately, she took out John Watson's half-crown. We know it was John Watson's half-crown for no one else could have afforded that sum of money. We knew that the Doc knew what she had done for he always gave himself away on such occasions by scratching his Tammany Nominee.

"There is something happening," commented the ever-wise Teke.
"What makes you say that?" asked the less astute, Gomez.
"The Doc scratched his Tammany Nominee."
"What does it mean?"
"It has something to do with our Mammy. I'm going to watch if he does it again when she goes up to his hut to pay for the papers."
Teke kept a discrete eye on the Doc's hut:
"Look, look! He did it; I seen his hand go down. He scratched his Tammany Nominee. It must have something to do with her."
There was a long discussion between our mother and the Doc but as she left he shouted after her:
"I'll make sure this winds up in the right place," and he again scratched his Tammany Nominee."

Mentioning John Watson brings another tale or two to mind. John was a big man and in more ways than just size; I don't know of anyone who ever crossed him. Ah! Except for one: Teke, my brother. We gathered potatoes for as little as nine pence per hour when we lived in the old homestead and one shilling and three pence per hour after we went to live in the new house. At the end of a six-day week, at the highest rate, we boys were coming out with almost three pounds in our grubby little pockets. This, of course, went straight into the coffers of the Targe and we would be lucky to receive two shilling or so back. We made sure it was spent very quickly, or she would borrow it back on a permanent loan basis. My usual investment was gob-stoppers, which I quickly sucked each one until the dye disappeared and ensured she could not return them to Mister Keene for a refund. I could them spend the next few days slobbering from the gob and unable to answer questions. I just shook my head pointed to the great bulge in my cheeks when someone wanted information.

One day little Teke counted his wages and found himself to be a shilling short. Off he set over the farmyard after a retreating 'Big John Watson.' "You've done me in a bob," he yelled at the top of his voice as he caught up with the respected farmer.

Although his little sandy head was about level with Big John's elbow, he grabbed the big man by the braces and stopped him in his tracks:

"You owe me another bob."

I was expecting a big hairy hand to swipe the lugs of my little brother, but that is not what happened. John Watson turned, planted his feet squarely, put his big hairy thumbs down the waist-band of his trousers and stared down at my brother. I do believe Roald Dahl based hid 'Bone Crunching Giant' from the story 'The BFG' on big John Watson.

"What did you say, young fellow?"

"I'm a bob short in my wages. You done me in a bob. Hand it over."

The big farmer was not used being spoken to like that. Nor, was he noted for his sense of humour, but I noticed that there was a slight indication of a smirk on his face and it took him a while to respond to the cheeky little urchin in short pants. Eventually, he said: "Come on into the house Paddy till we count up these calculations."

Fifteen minutes later the cheeky, sandy-haired blighter came out tossing a coin in his tiny, dirty hand. It was a bob.

I mentioned that John Watson was not exactly renowned for his sense of humour; well, one day he was to prove that point. I was feeding a thresher with corn sheaves which were being pitched to me by a man called Eugene Quinn. Eugene, never the greatest of friends with Big John, was standing about level with me. He was on a stack that he had already taken the top off. He lifted the big rope that had been used to tie

down the stack and pretended to gnaw it like a rat – just to make me laugh. Unfortunately, Eugene did not see John Watson watching him. John did not see me from where he stood so as far as he was concerned this wasn't a joke; this was a hungry man:
He shook his old head, took off his cap and scratched the baldy patch muttering: "That bloody man needs an extra spud or two come dinner time."

After the missing bob affair, Big John became my brother's 'new best friend' and they could be seen everywhere, talking about things, such as; the weather, the harvest and how much hogget were expected to fetch at Alam's sales. The conversation must have got around to football for the next thing was: Teke was off home to fetch the caser. What had happened was: John has asked my brother how far he could kick a football.
"Farther than you," was the reply.
Now, John Watson, some thirty years earlier played for a team of 'cloggers' (players who don't care whether they get the ball or miss it and get a scrotum instead – as long as it is a ball of some description). The team was called Slans United, and it was between him and his brother, George, as to who could hit a ball the hardest.

He wasn't likely to accept that a little runt in short pants could kick a ball further than he could even though it had been a long time since his playing days.

Dinner time meant a break from gathering the potatoes when a big aluminium milk-canister of tea arrived on the trailer that was being used to cart the potatoes back to an outhouse for storage. The canister would be accompanied by a potato basket filled with bread and jam sandwiches. Sanitation was a word in the dictionary and had nothing to do with the potato-gatherers, so everyone got tucked in with dirty, stinking, rotten hands and everything tasted dead-on. After 'dinner' was served and consumed the caser was produced.

Big John Watson took the first kick after he had shouted: "Best of three, Paddy!"

He kicked it about fifty or fifty-five yards. My little brother stepped up and kicked the ball over twice as distance. John improved on his next kick by a couple of yards or so:

"There's no point in you taking another go, Paddy, until I beat your first kick," Big John altered the rules in desperation.

His third kick fell short of his first one and shortly after that my brother was spinning another shiny bob coin is his pudgy hand whilst Big John just kept on feeling his once powerful legs, which were, by that time, over sixty years old.

Teke got himself a job as a trainee store-man in the Berkshire, a USA nylon stocking manufacturer based in Newtownards. It wasn't long before he hit on a scheme which brought him in a considerable sum until it too was 'twigged on'. One day a van drew up as Teke was manning the reception window:

"Hello! I wonder if you can help me young man."

"What can I do for you?" my brother asked, very politely for he was adept at spotting an opportunity even before it presented itself.

"I was wondering if you had any spare cardboard boxes, I'm in the export business, myself." Bad mistake for now our Paddy saw himself as being in the import business – importing some of his new best friend's cash into his cosy little pockets.

"It will cost you!" Paddy replied.

"How much?"

"Tanner a box."

"Threepenny-bit each."

"Done: how many do you need?"

"A hundred – for a start."

"A hun .. a hun .. " Paddy couldn't believe his ears, "that'll be three .. three .. hundred .."
"Two pounds and eight pence: shall we call it two pounds? And that price will go for future consignments."
"Future con .. consignments .. yes, yes, of course, of course we can call it two pounds," my brother stuttered.
The Boxer – as he became known held out his hand: "Who shall I call you?"
"Patrick! My name is Mister Patrick!" Well, who can blame him; I mean 'Patrick' does have a more entrepreneur ring to it than mere 'Paddy' and several times better than 'Teke'.

Everything went well for a considerable period of time but, like all good things, it had to end: My brother proved to be quite sharp and efficient at his job. This fact came to the notice of one of the floor managers who attempted to recruit him as a 'topper' – a person who machines the tops for nylon stockings.
"But the job pays twice as much as a store-man's assistant!" the floor manager told the boy who had suddenly become Patrick.
"No it doesn't!" my brother sighed within.
"So you are not interested, Paddy?"
"Patrick, if you don't mind."

"So you are not interested, Patrick?"

"No, not really."

And that is the way it stood until the day the Boxer met the chief executive of Berkshire Ireland Ltd at a civic function in Newtownards Towm Hall. "I see your young director, Mister Patrick is not here, I was hoping to extend our contract for the cardboard boxes," the Boxer took the opportunity to do more business.

"Patrick, young director! Cardboard boxes! Contract!" the chief executive of Berkshire Ireland Ltd got redder and redder in the face at the thought of the extra money that could be lining his own pocket.

It was a matter of either being shown the gate or becoming a topper and within the week, my brother was sitting behind his little topping machine. Being a nylon stocking topper served a purpose in later life as he had a ready-made excuse for examining the tops of ladies' stockings - for dropped stitches I presume.

A big, old man who lived about a mile away from our house worked in the nylon factory as a cleaner. One day he asked Teke if he fancied a lift back and forward to work on his motorbike. My brother jumped at the chance of saving on bus fares. The old man was known locally as

'County Cloughey'. Although Paddy came home with County Cloughey that evening, he got himself the bus the following morning, so I posed the question:

"Could you not have travelled every day with County Cloughey; it would have saved you on bus fares?"

"Let me tell you why I will never be on that motorbike in my life again. He stopped at every corner and tooted his bloody horn and when he came to road junctions, I had to hold the motorbike while he scanned up and down the bloody road to see if there was anything coming. As you can imagine; the bus, I should have been on, came up behind us; it was Vincent Fitzsimmons and he tooted at County Cloughey, knowing what to expect. But I didn't: County Cloughey drove into the next driveway to let the bus pass, and that's what happened with everything that overtook us, and if he couldn't find a driveway a gate into a field done just as well. It was nearly dark when we got home and I had to make a beeline for the flush-toilet."

No book would be worth its salt if it didn't mention the importance of a flush-toilet (water-closet) in those days. The first notable change was: the little loop of bailer-twine, which had hung on the outside toilet wall, holding together neat cut squares from the Irish News was replaced by something called a 'toilet roll' which was slotted into a device called a 'toilet-roll holder.' The novelty didn't last long for me as the Targe took it upon herself to stand outside the toilet door and count the number of pieces of toilet paper I used. From then on I could be observed taking with me, the advertisement page from the Irish News and a big pair of scissors. My God, you must be entitled to some degree of privacy. My ass must have looked like a blotter with the latest editions of births, deaths and marriages together with adverts and bankrupt columns but when the Doc got to hear about the development and asked to check out for 'Ford vans,' he was quickly turned down.

After the County Cloughey fiasco, Teke decided he would buy a little motorbike and the morale of the next story is: do not become a trainee pillion passenger with a trainee motorcyclist. Teke and I were more often in ditches than we were on the roads. On one particular occasion he was giving me a lift to my mate, Sean Caughey's house when the Doc spied us and tried to keep up with Ireland's answer to Geoff Duke. The junction between the Bog Road and Ballyeasboro Road is almost ninety degrees and we tried to take it at sixty miles per hour. I say us but really, I had no option in the matter. The Doc related how he turned in after us but found no sign of us or the little motorbike and if it hadn't been for a geyser of steam rising from an adjacent sheugh he would have thought we were away beyond the next bend.

On a beautifully sunny Sunday, Teke and I decided to put on our best gear and ride around the Walter Shore in Portaferry and do a bit of posing for the local females. There is a big sweeping corner on that stretch of road and it seems to be never-ending. It ended for Teke and me though, for we must have been doing about twice the speed we should have been doing if we were to have any chance of negotiating that bend. One second we were on the road; the next second we were on the grass and the following second we were in the sea. After we trained the motorbike out of Strangford Lough and peeled the sea-weed from our new suits we fell someway short of what girls might imagine posers to look like. "Not to worry," Teke assured, "we will strip off and dry these clothes in the sun.

"People passing by will see our Tammany Nominees," I protested, "We don't want anyone peeping at our Tammany Nominees."

"Well. I wouldn't be too sure about that big brother, it's all down to whoever passes by I suppose."

After a couple of hours of me lying on my belly and my brother lying on his back our clothes were dry. After we had dressed Teke looked at the rusting old wreck of a ship which had been towed up the lough by Lee the ship salvagers and challenged: "Last man on board is a cissy." Up the old slimy, rusty chain we spieled till we were almost at the top. Unfortunately the anchor chain did not extend the full way to the capstan and the length of rotten old hawser that did could no longer take the strain and with two almighty splashes the would be posers were back in the drink.

It would be impossible to write a true account of events in Northern Ireland without touching on sectarianism; it affected everyone at some stage during their lives. The Unionist vote depended upon keeping sectarianism alive and well and anyone denying that Catholics were not discriminated against in that process was living in a different world. I lost a job as an apprentice draughtsman due to the managing director's hatred of Catholics. I was booked for silly bicycle offences by a particular policeman who lay in wait, every Saturday night for me cycling to Kircubbin picture house and I was convicted of a felony even after all those guilty of the offence told the resident magistrate that I had nothing to do with it. But, strange to say, I am glad I lost my job as a young draughtsman for it gave me the experience of working in a bookmaker's shop and led me into the life of 'odds' and eventually to quantum physics.

It was in the bookie's shop that I became the subject of such Mafiosi type language, from my boss, that I thought only existed in black-and-white films. When I was in my late teens, I got a job in a particular bookmaker's shop in Bankmore Street in Belfast. There wasn't a great deal doing on in winter days, so I decided to spruce things up a bit by inventing: what I called a 'spinning wheel' which, if I might add; had little to do with yarn and a lot to do with making me a few bob on the side. It was a big wooden disc, divided up into coloured sections, each section being represented by odds, which were compiled to ensure I made a fair profit provided I could get the first day over without a long priced winner coming up.

Honestly speaking I couldn't have afforded a big pay-out and would have had to have scampered off had such a thing happened. The bookmaker's clerks and indeed, the manager told me I would go bust inside the first hour and laughed at the idea of a young teenager taking on seasoned punters.

All went exceedingly well and my pockets got so heavy in silver and coppers that I had to get the manager to transfer it into pound notes quite frequently. But, very soon, Geordie Duff, the owner who worked upstairs realized his takings were down considerably. One day, in the middle of 'raking it in' I looked up to see a horrible sight; a big fat baldy head occupied a pigeon hole usually reserved for one of the clerks. The beady eyes in that shiny head were focused on me and my little spinning board. The handle of the door, that separated the office from the pitch, turned and there stood my worst nightmare:
"Pay the man!" Geordie Duff calmly instructed.
I looked down to see that the wheel had stopped on an outsider which a regular punter had backed. I fumbled, coughed and spluttered but eventually managed to pay the grateful punter. The bookie lifted my wheel and ordered me to follow him upstairs to his office.

George Keenan (his real name – Duff was his business name as he was in the 'shady game') sat down and pointed for me to stand at the other side of his desk, cleared his throat and began,
"They all though you would lose money, but you are a smarter wee fucker that we had given you credit for, but you're not as smart as this baldy auld fucker here who has been in the game for nigh on forty years."
"Sorry Geordie!"
"Now, let me tell you why you are not as smart as you think you are. You shouldn't have mounted the bearing unto a second board for I considered dismantling it and adding a couple of magnets – one to the wheel and one to the board – and then wiring the punters off."
"You knew where the board was hidden at nights then?"
"There's fuck all that goes on here, that I don't know about and you'd do well to remember that," he raised his voice and I stepped back a pace or so.
"You're not going to sack me then?"
"No," he shook his massive baldy head, "But you will not need wages for a month or so and I'm sure my calculations are correct."
"Thank you, Geordie!"

George Keenan did not deduct one penny from my wages, but I never saw my trusty spinning-wheel again.

Earlier, in these writings, I promised to give an explanation as to where the phenomena of the great fire in the aerodrome had its origins: Readers will recall my description of 'The Gorbals' in relation to my great-grandmother and her son, my grandfather. It came to be that I stood in the Gorbals of Glasgow about the time they were just starting to pull it down. The colourless black and grey tenement squalor with their steep cold steps disappearing up into the drizzly mist involved my mind so deeply with the past that I could have really been there in those times when the residents of those slums, including my great-grandmother were treated little better than pigs. Some of those towering buildings were blackened by fire but probable the majority had been set ablaze by kids, alcoholics or drug addicts. It was one such burned-out building with its jagged black rafters sticking into the sky like devil's fingers of confusion that startled me to the core. It resembled the building my mate and I witnessed in that inferno in Kirkistown Aerodrome.
"Oh my God! We witnessed a playback!" I stood trembling on the spot. I wanted to flee.

That was the only thing on my mind. It had something to do with me, perhaps a personal hell. The great lesson was: we live in a 'timeless now' and we only differentiate the past from the present from the future in order that our individualization makes reasonable sense to a memory that is structured upon harmonious unity (the mind of God.) There are those out there in the vast expanses of our universe who can record and play back events in a similar, but much more sophisticated manner, to our recording of live events and play-back on a monitor. They energise atmospheric gasses or water-vapour to play their holograms; perhaps, to remind us that we are not quite as important as we tend to think we are.

Everybody has their own private hell and there was one drunken cyclist who was taken through a living nightmare by me and a young lady of like mind. Just after midnight on a quiet country road leading past an ancient graveyard a lonely cyclist meandered drunkenly from one side of the road to the other. The speed of the wheels barely turned the dynamo to light his headlamp. As he approached the graveyard, torturous moaning chilled his spine. He peered over the low graveyard wall and there amongst the headstones clearly saw a ghostly head and a blood-red hand, neither apparently attached to a body. Sobriety returned; his cycle straightened, and the light generated by the dynamo illuminated the road ahead for a good hundred yards. We were the only people who knew it was an illusion for we used two powerful torches to get the desired effect together with my friend's weird special sound of a skeleton moaning. But it didn't stop the drunk from telling the tale in the local pub the next time he went there and that story circulated for many years as 'supernatural truth'.

"We could set up a tidy spook business", my friend suggested some years later.

"Yea," I replied, "and have some nutcase in this god-dam place really make you moan when he decides to take a pot-shot at you."

My second little sister, Yvonne, the one we nicknamed, 'Wee Wong' decided she was going to defy family tradition and marry a protestant. She did, and Robert turned out to be a fine husband and I became very friendly with him. Robert had a subtle sense of humour and an example of that was: he got a new set of false teeth but complained that an excessive consumption of alcohol seemed to have loosened them. Texas Sam was driving us home at the time but came around a corner, at a fair rate of knots, only to find a car skidding broadside at us having come around the same corner from the opposite direction at much too high a speed. My youngest brother had no option but to plunge his car over the ditch. We landed with a great thump on the other side but, luckily enough; the car managed to stay on all four tyres.

"Them auld teeth fit better now," Robert commented as we dragged ourselves out of the car.

Another example of my brother-in-law's humour was; when his two young boys, Rodney and Gary, were in the back seat with me when we were driving through Wales on a rather frosty morning. We rounded a corner, in a village, and a little Taff took umbrage to Garry's Irish face and stuck his tongue out at my little nephew. Suddenly, Gary protested: "Daddy, that wee boy's sticking 'my' tongue out at me."

"Maybe he's trying to keep his own one warm, son," Robert told him and that was an end to the matter.

At week-ends, I used to take those two little children over the fields, the hills and the shore, and together we invented a place we called: 'The Happy Hunting Ground.' In the Happy Hunting

Ground quite ordinary features and ordinary occurrences took on mightily important roles, and I got as much pleasure from listening to their young and fertile minds as they did from our explorations. Their world of make-believe could not last forever for the Sword of Damocles hung above them; and when it fell, it cut their lives to pieces.

When the boys were still very young, their mother; my lovely, sister, died at the tender age of thirty-three. Wee Wong died in the operating theatre in the Royal Hospital in Belfast, whilst undergoing surgery for a tumour on her pituitary gland and for those two little lads the world never was the same again. Just before the operation she asked me if she would come through it all right as she trusted in my psychic ability. I took her in my arms and reassured her, but when she died, I could not understand why I had not had a premonition that all would not turn out well.
My wife shook her head in disbelief: "Do you mean to say you have forgotten the night you woke up sobbing about what would now happen to Robert and her two little boys?'
I had forgotten—up until she reminded me, but now I firmly believe we have a balancing memory mechanism that trip-switches' on occasions,

mostly for the better for how could I have told my little sister the truth or told her a lie? They kept her body artificially functioning by machines for far too long and day-after-day, night-after-night we kept vigil and I now know that the reason for doing so was: to match her donated organs up with suitable recipients. Surgeons and administrators of organ allocation must be brought to understand that there is a spiritual dimension involved in the process inasmuch as; as long as bodies are kept artificially alive the soul will not depart and is left in a state of limbo. When the machine was turned off, in the case of my little sister, I suddenly I felt a glorious peace descending from somewhere and settling all around me, and the words floated through my head: "She is free."

On my unscheduled return home from the County of Lancaster, I got a job in a firm called the Belfast Ropeworks Company Ltd. They had just opened a new site in a village called Ballygowan very close to where my mother was born. A shift system operated in the factory and there were eight foremen employed to run the manual end of the processing. The only one I reckoned had any brains at all was little Ricky Salmon and I soon got fed up with them making the wrong decisions and causing unnecessary work. With that in mind I asked one of the assistant managers, Tony Malone, if the foremen had to take any form of exam to gain their positions within the company. He rather sarcastically suggested I might consider setting out a paper to facilitate such an examination. It was probably the most stupid remark he ever made, for the challenge was taken up with a certain amount of gusto and here are some of the questions I set out:

1. In the space provided write a comprehensive essay on the health advantages of the beef-burger. (I allowed a space the size of a postage stamp)
2. From a nutritional point of view, explain in a word, or less, why the Irish bog oak was preferred to the common, peat-bog turf.
3. Give your opinion why Churchill did not call on the services of Admiral Lord Nelson in the campaign carries out by the Desert Rats.
4. In a game of noughts and crosses where would you put a single X to ensure your opponent could not win the game? In this particular instance, you opponent has five O's (a blank noughts and crosses diagram was provided).

5. Which one of the following is not a male animal: a) sporran, b) fig leaf, c) haggis
6. Arsenic is a component part of a magnet and which other food-stuff?
7. Who plays the Doldrums and which group do you associate him with?
8. Who discovered penicillin and how long did it take him stuffing it back into the tube?
9. How would a moccasin be best put to use? a) beating a squaw, b) walking to the South Pole, c) chastising a ferocious lioness that was eating your ham sandwiches.
10. Name the planet that is missing from this sequence; bus, overcoat, thingamabob ---?
11. If you had a choice, whose socks would you choose to wear at the Edinburgh Tattoo. Write his name here in Roman Numerals but please do not use capitals unless you think you have to in order to avoid breaking the law.

I think there were about fifty questions, but I can't remember any more. At least, two people tried to answer the questions and I made sure they arrived on the manager's desk. The only answers I remember are by a little man called Bill Colt and they were as follows:

Answer to number 1. = Beef/Bap

Answer to number 4. = He drew a massive big X, in thick marker, across the entire puzzle.

After Tony Malone left the company, I got a job as foreman but another one of the managers, Lennie Hogg, came to me and said: "You are lucky I wasn't on the interviewing panel, sending that fucking forklift driver 'round to see if I'd finished with the bloody Ganges Basin, I don't know."

A little man by the name of George Caughey joined the Belfast Ropeworks and I hit it off immediately with him. George was a man of high intelligence and as sharp as a new pin. There was a big fat man employed in the waste plastic reclaiming section and he was one of those people who thought he knew it all. It would not matter what the conversation was: he was an authority on it and a loud authority at that. George Caughey and I decided to 'bait' Big Daddy, as we called him. We didn't have to plan or rehearse anything as George was spontaneous. Unfortunately, at our dining table was a young lad with a big heart and a small brain. I opened the conversation:
"You were in the war, Geordie, what was it really like?"

"You always bring this topic up, you know I am very embarrassed by the whole affair," George responded.

I didn't have a clue where he was heading, but I tried to carry on: "Okay, so you got yourself into hot water but tell us all why?"

"Nobody told me!"

"Nobody told you what?"

"Nobody told me who to shoot at!"

"So, you were shooting away at your own men, right, left and centre," I shook my head.

"In training, our side wore blue arm-bands but that lot weren't wearing any blue arm-bands, so I thought they were fair game," George came back at me.

"Fair game! Fair fucking game, your own men!" Big Daddy rose to the bait as we knew he would.

"He didn't know. He didn't do it deliberately," the young lad with a big heart and a small brain came to George's defence, "he didn't get proper training."

"He wasn't paying proper attention, if you ask me. If you are given charge of a rifle it's up to you to learn how to handle the fucking thing," Big Daddy growled.

"How did you eventually catch on?" I tried to get George back in.

"That I was gunning down my own men, you mean?"

"Yea"

"My platoon sergeant came up to my dug-out and said: 'Excuse me!'"

"Fucking excuse me, and you're wiping out half the fucking platoon!" Big Daddy again interrupted.

"Maybe a bit more than half," George confessed putting his hands over his eyes in shame.

"He didn't know they were on his side," the young lad with a big heart and a small brain again came to George's defence, "that sergeant should have told him at the start."

"Carry on Geordie," I encouraged, "this sergeant came up to you, all casual like, prodded his finger into you and said: 'Excuse me.' What then?"

"That's exactly what he said: 'Excuse me, but you do seem to be whacking our own men. You had better have one bloody good excuse for this."

"And did you – have a bloody good excuse?" I asked.

"Not really, George Caughey shook his head, "but I did tell the sergeant that I thought something was not right when a corporal turned around to me and shouted, 'Hold your fire, Paddy!'"

"Was he speaking in English or German?"

"English, alright, but he said it with a Birmingham accent."

"So what conclusion did you come to?"

"Nothing really, I just thought it was a bit strange."

"So what did you do?"

"I shot him."

"I bet you he wasn't a happy bunny?"

"Happy, fucking bunny!" Big Daddy yelled out.

"Mister Caughey was right; you can't take chances in wars," the young lad with a big heart and a small brain looked Big Daddy straight in the eye.

"So, did that sergeant have you court-martialled then?" I kept it going.

"No, luckily enough, he was taken prisoner by a Stuka," George replied, doing well to supress a grin.

Big Daddy arose and bent over the table towards George Caughey, until their two faces nearly met: "A Stuka was a dive bomber, a fucking Junkers eighty-seven. Don't you mean a Hun? A fucking Hun captured your mate."

"He was no mate of mine," George protested.

"Lucky for him," I suggested, "for being a mate of yours could have fatal consequences by your own admission."

"Did the Germans let him go after the war was over," enquired the young lad with a big heart and a small brain.

"No, he was never heard of again."

"Maybe he was from Birmingham," I shook my head in sympathy.

"Ah, perhaps you are right. Maybe justice was done in the long run," George agreed.

"Did you get any medals for bravery or anything like that," I prompted.

"Unfortunately no, well none from our side any-how," George sighed, "Herr Villi Brant wanted to award me the Iron Cross, Second Class, after he became Chancellor when the war was over but nothing much came of it."

"Fucking right, nothing much would come of it. Can you not imagine what the fucking papers would say? Churchill and Monty and them boys from Whitehall are smarter than you, Sunshine," Big Daddy had the last word as we hoped he would.

I mentioned a little man called Bill Colt. Well, he was one of the most annoying characters you could ever meet; on the level of Big Daddy but in a different way. Colt was everywhere that he shouldn't be and nowhere that he should be. If you were doing something say, for example, something that was 'bad practice' (for the want of a better phrase), Bill Colt would catch you. If you had brought a machine down due to neglect, Bill Colt would be there with comforting words, such as: "I knew that was going to happen, you should make sure you have enough granules in the hopper or that will happen." Ricky Salmon, another foreman, was particularly affected by Colt's sudden apparitions. One particular day Ricky was a bit off colour and was spooning through his soup with little interest of actually putting the spoon into his mouth, when the engineer asked him: "What are you looking for in that bowl of soup, Ricky?

"Fucking Bill Colt, the wee bollocks has been everywhere else today," he replied.

"I know what we should do with him," I got a bit excited with my own thoughts.

"What?" asked a rather nonchalant Ricky?

"Put him on trial the next time wee Geordie Caughey is on the same shift as us on overtime."

And here is how it happened; Gorge Caughey agreed to be judge, Ricky Salmon was to prosecute and I got to defend the little shit. I would much rather have been prosecuting or judging and only agreed on the role if the other two let me be hangman as well. We piled into the canteen when Bill Colt was seen to go in carrying his neat little lunch box. However, who happened to be already there but Big Daddy. There was simply no way we would be able to carry out our little scheme without the big man's interference.

George Caughey went up to Bill Colt, laid his hand on the little man's shoulder and asked, "Is your name Bill Colt?"

"Yes but what are you playing at now, Geordie?"

"I have a warrant here for your arrest."

He had, and it had an official looking RUC police heading to it.

"The Court decrees that you may eat during proceedings provided your food is not crisps or other noisy substances."

"Such as tomato ketchup," I added.

"I don't know where you have been, but tomato ketchup was not very crunchy the last time I had some," Big Daddy interrupted.

"The Court rules in favour of the big man here," then George turned to me, "If you are going to defend that little piece of shit there, then you must really learn to be able to distinguish between potato crisps and sauce."

"I'm sorry, M' Lud!"

George pulled a chair up in front of Bill Colt and cleared his throat several times.

"What are you playing at, what is all this bluttering and coughing about?" Bill Colt wanted to know.

"All judges do that, especially when they are constipated," Geordie replied.

"What the fuck has clearing your throat got to do with constipation?" Big Daddy asked.

"I'm sorry; I bow to the Learned Council's information."

"I'm not your Learned Council; I am just keeping you right from a medical point of view."

"Thank you, thank you, now who brings this case against the accused, Bill Guilty-as-Hell, Colt?" the judge asked.

"Are judges not supposed to be neutral?" asked Big Daddy.

"I was in neutral but I have gone up a gear."

"Funny, fucking very funny, but if you are going to play these silly games at least get your facts straight."

Ricky Salmon got to his feet: "I charge this wee bollocks with being a spy for British Ropeworks. He gets all our plastic mixtures and writes them down on a piece of paper and then sends them to British Ropeworks."

“Who appears for the defence of this little traitor?” the judge asked.
I arose, bowed gracefully and replied: “I do, M’ Lud.”
“Does your client plead guilty or not guilty?”
“The little creep pleads guilty M’ Lud.”
“I fucking don’t!” Colt shouted.
“Objection overruled.”
George Caughey then took from his pocket a black rag he had found in the fitter's shop which was meant for soaking up grease. He put it on his head and asked: “Is there a hangman in the building?”
“Indeed, M’ Lud,” I again bowed.
“Mister Pierrepiont,” I order you to take this man here to a place in a lawful prison, and thence from such lawful prison to a place of execution wherein you will hang this man by the neck until he is dead.”
I made a move towards little Bill Colt but at that moment, he leapt to his feet and flew out of the door like Linford Christie with a dose of the runs.

Not-to-worry, when I returned unto the shop floor, I decided to take matters a step further; after the office staff went home; I went into the rope section and found myself a piece of heavy hawser, some four inches thick, and made a hangman's noose out of it. I threw it over a beam then went into the elevated office and kept a watch on Bill Colt. He kept looking at the noose and back at me but otherwise went on with his work at his extrusion machine. Then I upped the ante by drawing up a notice giving the time of the 'Official Hanging'.

"He's only kidding, isn't he?" Colt asked Ricky Salmon.

"Kidding! You don't know that bloody man," Ricky replied, "sure it was him that rode a circus elephant into a card school and all because he lost two bob at a game of snap."

With that Bill Colt took off again but this time, he stood outside the big door for the remainder of the shift, leaving Ricky and I to doff his machine every couple of hours.

"That'll teach you not to play silly games," Big Daddy smirked as he walked past on his way to the drink's machine where he seemed to spend half of every shift.

Working with Big Daddy, on the waste reclamation machines was a little nut-case called Dickey John. When he thought that he had done enough for the night he usually climbed into a big cardboard box and dozed off. On night-shift it was part of my responsibility to make sure those boys were doing their share so I used to kick the cardboard box as I walked past not being over particular what my boot connected with. Dickey John knew there was no point in retaliating or even protesting as he'd wind up 'kicking stones' on his way home to an early kip but he still kept doing it. One shift Ricky and I found him snoring away in a cardboard box which was sitting on a pallet. I eased the fork-lift truck into the pallet and lifted Dickey John and his box fourteen feet into the air and left him there. Towards the end of the shift he began to climb out before realising that he couldn't find a foot-hold underneath and promptly returned into the box.

"All you need is a pair of wings and you'd make a good crow," Ricky hollered up at him.

Dickey John repaid my bad deed with a good deed when he came to my assistance one evening after a steel bar had fallen unto my head. Although it knocked me to my knees and the blood was streaming down my face, I really didn't feel any pain. Dickey John was awake at the time and ran over to me carrying his favourite chair. He shouted to anyone who got in his way: "Get out of the road, that man's head's cut."

I am sure there were many employees who were in total agreement with that statement. Dickey John got me seated and examined my head:
"There is one hell of a hole there," he concluded. I was okay before he examined me, but suddenly, I felt really sick and had thoughts of medical people, in white coats, pushing me, on a trolley, like the hammers of hell down some hospital corridor; and all those sorts of things.

About this time, I started going out with the girl I eventually married. I took her over to Bristol to introduce her to my brother, the one we called Teke and his wife, Sheila. My brother had built a shed in his back garden and my girlfriend remarked on how nice it was; well, she could hardly say it was a bit crappie looking, could she?
"Is that where they kept their little dog?" she enquired of me.
"Yes, that was Taddles' little home before he passed on," I replied; forgetting to tell her that 'Taddles' was the name Sheila's father was best known by; in fact, their dog was called Brandy. Bye and bye, there came the time when Sheila and my future wife were together in the back garden.

"That is a wonderful shed your good husband has built. He is quite good with his hands," my girlfriend sucked up to her host.

"Yes, we wanted something special."

"Did Taddles sleep in it all his life or did you allow him to stay in the house during thunder and lightning and things?"

"Taddles stayed in the house all the time he was here, I'll have you know."

"Sorry, it's just that I saw his bowl in there. Did you just put it out there after he passed away?"

"Taddles ate at the table with the rest of us, not down on his knees on the bloody floor."

"Aught, that was nice of you. Did he sit up in a chair with his little bib on?"

"Excuse me, but are you trying to be funny? Why wouldn't I treat my father like all the rest of the family?"

"Taddles is your father's name!"

"Who the hell did you think he was - the bloody dog?"

"I'll kill that shit!"

A little man called Leo joined the Belfast Rope-works and was put to work on a device that extruded PVC clothes-line. One day he came to me to complain:

"I'm going to shut that machine down, put my coat on and go home."
"Are you not going to tell me why you have decided on that course of action?"
"They have started calling me 'wanker' here too."
"What do you mean 'here to' where else did they call you that?"
"They called me that in the mill. That's why I left."
"You didn't perhaps; relate that information to anyone here?"
"I warned everybody when I started here that if they called me 'wanker' I'd hit them a dig in the gob."
"That would go some way to explaining why they now refer to you in such terms."
"Well, I've had enough of it."
I put my hand on his shoulder: "I tell you what, Leo; if you keep that machine running I will go across and hit a couple of them with a shovel."
"Do you not want to know who called me that name so that you can hit the right ones?"
"No, it doesn't matter, Leo, I'm not fussy who I hit. One of them girls over there will do to start with. It will teach them all a lesson."
"No, don't hit one of the wee girls – it wasn't them."

I lifted a shovel used in the plastic granules bin and having gathered several operatives around me before I started whacking it off the doffing table like I'd just gone crazy. Of course all the operatives were 'in the know.'

"Hey WANKER, I shouted across at Leo."

He pointed at his own chest and replied, "What, me?"

"Yes, you come here!"

Over he came.

"I've just told these nut cases here that if anyone one of them calls you 'wanker' again I will ram this shovel up his ass."

"Thank you," and off he sauntered happily to his machine.

It didn't solve the problem entirely, but it gave Leo the satisfaction of responding: "The foreman will shove a shovel up your arse if you call me that again."

In the late seventies, I went to work, again as a foreman, with the ill-fated Delorean Company and got off to a really fortunate start. Ten years earlier I had applied for a job in the Ford Factory at Halewood, near Liverpool and had sat an examination. All applicants who had sat the exam that day met in the canteen and discussed the paper and found out where we had gone wrong and vice-versa, of course. You can imagine my surprise when I sat the exam for Delorean and opened the first page to find that it was the same paper I had sat at Halewood those ten years earlier. Mr Hundred per cent I was referred to later – if only they had known.

I was lucky not to have been sacked almost as soon as I joined that company. Each of us had to do a training video in which we acted as salesmen for the 'Gull-winged, Delorean sports car.' After doing a proper recording, which, I must add, wouldn't have got me a job giving away soft paper tissue, at a railway station toilet, my big mate and I scripted a 'funny' version during lunch break and put it on tape. It went something like this:
Knock, knock!
"Good morning madam," I acted as the salesman.
"Good morning," my mate acted as the recipient of a cold call.
"I see you are an old age pensioner."
"That's right; now what the fuck do you want?"
"I see you drive a little Morris Minor. Would you like to swap it for a brand new, gulled-winged, Delorean sports car?"
"Why should I? My wee Morris Minor is better than them sports car thingamabobs."

"You are probably right there, Madam but when the wheels fall off your little Morris Minor as they regularly do with the Delorean sports car, especially going around corners, your car can't sprout wings and take to the air – can it?"

"If I wanted to fly I'd buy a fucking aeroplane; one of them wee Cecil things for me and the auld man, wouldn't I?"

"Cessna, I think you mean – you stupid auld bat."

At this point we were laughing so much at our own jokes, we had to rewind the tape and do part of it again.

It continued as such:

"So what do you think Madam of my offer?" I continued.

"I think you are trying to get into my knickers!"

"Fuck off Dave, that's not in the script."

"Okay, okay, what's next?"

"About the size of the wheels," I prompted.

"Oh aye, yes! Why has your sports car thingy got two big wheels on the back and two small wheels on the front?"

"Because if we had put one big wheel and one wee wheel on the front and a big wheel and a wee wheel on the back it would have bumped all over the place like a fucking camel with gout, wouldn't it, you brainless auld tart?"

"It said on the telly, that there is no steel in them there roll bars. They are all made out of that puffed candy stuff."

"That, Madam, is called foam, equally as strong as the best of British steel."

"Pity."

"What do you mean?"

"If you broke down in the desert or the outback or somewhere like that you could always break a bit off and have a snack, if it had been made from puffed candy, I mean."

"Look Madam, this car wasn't designed to get any further than to the ship in Belfast docks and get it away from the prying eyes of the government."

"So, you are saying that if I wanted to take a trip to the desert or outback I couldn't?"

"What the fuck does an auld bitch like you want in the desert or the bloody outback, for that matter?

There was much more to it than this but, once again, I have forgotten most of it.

We intended showing the other trainee foremen the video on the next day's lunch break but for some unknown reason one of the instructors decided to play it back before packing the equipment away for the night and he reported it to

senior management. News got through to us that the 'big noises' were on their way to view it in a private room so a spy was sent out to listen in as I prepared my defence.
He came back and reported: "They are laughing their fucking heads off."
We heard no more about it.

The younger instructor at Delorean was very fond of his flip-charts and was very good at milking his pupils for all they were worth; resulting in him having to contribute very little to each lesson.
"What would a foreman expect from his operatives?" he asked, with his stout marker at the ready.
"Effort," suggested one of the trainee foremen.
"Very good," and he wrote it on the flip chart.
"Dedication," another suggested.
"Excellent" and he wrote that down too.
"Good time keeping"
"Yes, indeed."
"Passion," I ventured
"Yes, a deep dedication for his work," the young instructor miss-interpreted my word so that it became acceptable.
"Love," I tried again.

"Love?" my mate shouted out, "Nobody, in their right mind loves their foreman; more like they hate him."

"What about the crawlers?" I asked.

The instructor compromised by adding both the words 'Love' and 'Hate' to his chart.

But I wasn't too happy with that, so I further suggested: "Assistance with his toiletries."

"Be more specific, please."

"Ass-licking."

He actually wrote down: 'licking.'

"And what would an operative expect from his foreman?" he asked, mostly to change the subject.

"Fairness," the man across from me shouted out.

"Fairness," the instructor repeated as he wrote it down.

"Assistance," another suggested and it too was written down.

"Help," suggested someone who wasn't paying enough attention so the young instructor put a back-slash behind 'Assistance' and added the word 'Help.'

"A beating," I ventured.

"A beating?" the instructor queried.

"Yes, like when his work is not really up to standard," I tried to look as serious as I could under the circumstances.

"Did you beat-up your workers when you are a foreman at the Ropeworks?" my big mate kept it going.
"Only when it cost the firm money," I retorted. I couldn't believe my eyes when the young instructor intervened: "Alright, gentlemen, thank you, thank you," and wrote down the word : 'Reprimand.'
"He is going to go places," I concluded when he is able to take that kind of nonsense and still carry on.

My wife had five children altogether, but two of the infants died after living only one day on this earth. The other three did us proud through academic qualifications, but that is not what I wish to write about in this little book. Each of my three boys contributed to my firm belief in reincarnation, through three completely different occurrences.

My eldest living child, Aaron was about three years of age, when he astonished my wife and I when he said to me: "You were not my only daddy you know. My other daddy left us when the soldiers came. He left us and went up into the hills and we never seen him again. My second living child, Marcus has memories of what

sounds like a primeval landscape with fire and black lava and little or no vegetation. This convinces me that he is a relatively new spirit to this dimension.
My third living child, asked us about: “A man all dressed in brown that keeps coming down through the roof every time the priest lifts his arms up in the air.”
I explained to him that what he had witnessed was the Spirit of a monk from bygone days who was so obsessed with the ‘Consecration’ part of the ‘Mass’ that he became earth-bound.

On the subject of attending the Catholic Church: one day I asked Lee did he know the little family who always seated themselves in the front pew. He shook his little head and replied: “I don’t know them, Daddy; I think they must be protestants.”

In nineteen-eighty, we moved to Larne to start up a factory engaged in manufacturing a gambling game I had invented. We employed about thirty people at one time, but reliability let us down and eventually the firm went to the wall. That necessitated me in taking a security job with the local harbour and this suited me fine as, in quiet periods, I was able to continue in my pursuit of games invention. I held several 'letters patent' but had to do all the patent work myself as I couldn't afford professional fees. Around the same time, I found it necessary to learn computer programming so that I could better demonstrate my ideas in animated formation.

I soon made friends with three gentlemen from the harbour who were the life and soul of the party and if it hadn't been for them the place would have been one miserable dump. They were: John McManus, the 'Old Stretcher Bearer'; Charlie Murray, the 'Captain's Mate and John Moore, the 'Auld 10p Guard'. The man who ran the place, as Harbour Master, was the type of person who would have been 'head-hunted' by Reinhard Heydrick. He went out of his way to check that all the security guards were properly wet if it happened to be raining; otherwise they were deemed not To be doing their job properly.
One day the Old Stretcher Bearer said to me:
"Look we are going to have to bring a bit of culture to this place."
"That's what is lacking," I replied, "I trust it is a matter of growing something in a dirty tin for I can't see us having any other sort of influence on this lot."

"A poetry book, where everyone can contribute their own verses; that's the answer," my friend suggested.

"Huh, I don't envisage a poet laureate emerging from that mob."

"But that the beauty of it. There will be more laughs than words of profound wisdom."

"Yes, I see what you mean."

So we set the ball in motion.

Within a month, the book was crammed full. There was a varied mixture of wit, sentimentality and genuine inspiration but ninety per-cent of it was absolute rubbish. The Old Stretcher Bearer was right; it really lifted the whole place and there were times when he and I couldn't get to the end of some poems for collapsing in laughter. One lady, who saw herself as being 'saved' (one of the chosen few), objected to the vulgarity of some of the work but a young harbour policeman asked her why, if one particular piece, was so offensive, she had read it three times? The beauty of the venture was; there was nothing the sad Harbour Master could do about our happiness, although it must be admitted, we strived to put on a long face when he came our way.

Ode to the Harbour Lauriat (an example of one of our poems)

He stood in the rain
That drove others insane
And dreamt of his days with the Harriers
Whilst pointing the way
To the tourists each day
He played wonderful tunes on the barriers

Blown outside-in
And soaked to the skin
He danced to keep out the cold
He handed out books
To saints and to crooks
And saluted the Captain - I'm told

But just like the rest
He came to detest
The Captain and most of his crew
But it came with a jolt
When he planned a revolt
Amongst a mutinous few

There – with Eamon and Glen
And Will O' the Pen
And Moore from an old people's home
They wrote and they scribed
With Colin imbibed
And sunk the Old Port with a poem

A tall, skinny man called Lennie joined us some time later. Lennie was fond of a drink; a good drink and as a result often arrived at work the 'morning after' with a thick head. One such morning I noticed that he was somewhat the worst of the weather and on top of that, his gate was particularly busy. He was staggering from one place to the other, issuing passes, collecting tickets, filing documents from goods vehicles and dealing with enquiries. In other words, Lennie was snowed under. I decided it might be a good time to add to his problems with a telephone call.

The phone rang for some time before he could find time to answer it and to do that he had to close down both gates:

"Hello," he yelled.

"Lennie?"

"Yes, who the hell do you think it is?"

"I can see you are a bit busy but this is quite important."

"Get on with it."

"Lennie, are you aware that Nabucco and Nebuchadnezzar are one and the same person?"

"Listen mate, if you have any more of them words of wisdom, I'm sure you wouldn't mind keeping them to your fucking self," said he, my new, ex-friend, Lennie, slamming down the phone.

The contract was run by a little man from Scotland called Colin (as mentioned in the poem above). One morning he was giving me a hand by collecting tickets from lorries coming off the commercial ferry-boat.

"Hi, Jimmy! Jimmy, can you tell me the way to Ballymena" a fellow Scot yelled at Colin.
"How did you know my name was Jimmy?"
"I just guessed it, mate."
"Well you can guess the way to fucking Ballymena for you seem to be good at it?"
"That was a bit risky," I interrupted.
"Not really," he replied, "I've just been offered a similar job in Scotland.

The biggest prank we pulled was, unfortunately, at the expense of my mate – the Auld 10p Guard. Out of modelling clay I crafted an excretion of excruciating proportions. This was quite fitting (excuse the pun) for the man whom the blame was directed at had a posterior to match anyone using the ships, if not the ships themselves. Part of the art-work consisted of three or four pieces

of toilet paper, so it could be said, with all due modesty: "It really looked the part."
The offensive object was placed behind some, scraggy, low bushes, which were very close to the security hut but well within sight of road users. We arranged for a lorry driver to point the bluff excrement out to the Auld 10p Guard. He, in turn, pointed it out to the Old Stretcher Bearer, the Captain's Mate and me. Of course, we acted quite flabbergasted.

Phase one was out of the way but now began phase two:
I scanned a company letter heading and prepared what appeared to be an official notice which went something like this:
Our customer has brought to the notice of the company a serious infringement of regulations regarding hygiene and in particular the non-usage of toilet facilities within the harbour confines. Excrement was found within sight and smell of customers using the harbour entrance at the South Gate. Our scientific laboratories found that the substance matter was of human origin and of such dimensions that it had to be the product of a particularly large gluteus maximus.
Our department of criminology has investigated the matter and have taken statements to the effect

that a heavily built man, probably in his late fifties and wearing a bright yellow coat of the security variety was seen in the act of exposing such sized gluteus maximus. Several of those giving statements suggested that the large man cleansed himself after the act whilst another believed that it was a security guard with a fat face and a large nose, resting on his chin whilst waving a handkerchief at people entering and leaving the harbour. The management wishes to point out that such indiscretion will not be tolerated and will carry out a swab test on all employees answering to the aforementioned description.
Please append signatures on the dotted lines below:

"Did you see that letter in the canteen?" I asked the Auld 10p Guard.
"I did, I did and I don't think much of it."
"Why?"
"There's only me and a couple of others that fit that description."
I breathed deeply to try to suppress a laugh before adding: "I don't believe that bit about someone resting his chin on the ground and waving at people; do you?"
"Maybe he was crying."
"What makes you say that?"

"It would bring tears to anybody's eyes; doing one that size, wouldn't it?"
I shook my head: "Maybe a bloody dog did it – who knows?"
"That was done by a human being; I know human shit when I see it."
"You are probable right. I wouldn't have the same expertise in that particular field as your good self."
"I don't know about that, but one thing I do know is …"
"What's that?"
"I'll be doing no signing if they are only going to investigate people with big arses"

Although I had been a policeman, the Old Stretcher Bearer would have been a far more observant man than I and it was for that reason he was given the job of watching to see if he could find out why certain items were disappearing from the harbour. For the task, he was allocated a little hut that was part of the small toilet system. He couldn't understand why the lorry drivers were giving the place a wide berth even though he had taken all measures possible to conceal his presence. He only twigged on when the Captain's Mate informed him that I had sneaked up and chalked upon the wall the words; 'The Cottage'.

In the town, I lived in for most of my married life; my local was called the Railway Bar. Over the years, I had lots of fun in that establishment but the one that sticks out in my memory involved an old tramp called Mile Bush May. She had such a shrill, unintelligible voice that I used her as another leading character in ‘Plonkton.’ Mile Bush May was barred from every pub in the town and every pub in most of the towns within a fifty mile radius. She used to hang about the pubs watching for the landlord or landlady leaving and then sneak in, in the hope that whoever was serving on would not know she was barred. The first time I ever saw Mile Bush May she was trying to conceal herself against the gable wall of the Railway Bar and I mistook her for a mop.

“What the hell are you doing, hiding in there,” I asked her.

“Would you jist fetch me a wee surp o’ Guinness, Sir?”

“Come into the bar and I’ll buy you a drink.”

“Oh, I canny do that, Sir, fer that auld man in there hates me guts.”

I went into the bar and ordered a pint of lager;

“And a bottle of Guinness please.”

"You're very welcome to the pint, but you're not buying drink for that dirty auld bitch out there," the landlord growled.

"How did you know I was getting the Guinness for her?"

"Look, I was born in Ballymena – not Bally James fucking Duff."

That settled the matter for that particular day but provided me with ammunition for another.

Sometime later I was sitting at same bar when I saw a scraggy old mop head peeping around the door. The landlord wasn't there and the girl who was serving on had little experience, so I waved Mile Bush May in and bought her a bottle of Guinness. She had no sooner taken a few sups out of it than she started cackling and singing in such a high-pitched voice that I had to stick my fingers in my ears.

"Don't think much of your girlfriend," the young barmaid whispered to me.

Neither did the next man who came through the door – the publican:

"What in the name of fuck is that dirty auld bitch doing sitting there? I just hope she hasn't pissed herself where she sits."

"I didn't know she wasn't allowed in," the bar-maid apologised.

"No, but he did," he turned on me; "if you fetch that auld tramp in here again it's you who will be barred."

I promise to leave the subject of drunks if the reader will only digest this little gem that happened near my home quite recently. I am not sure how I would have dealt with this incident had I still been in the police force:
A man who lives a couple of block away from our house sat proudly on his little mobility scooter as he awaited his mates for a night out on the town. Both he and his little scooter were shined up so well that the 'disability touts' would have been reluctant not to report both to the dole for making false claims. Eventually off they set with the three mates pushing the DLA man up the hill that was testing the little mobility scooter to its limit.

About 1am there was a terrible ruction from up on the top of our road. I looked out of my bedroom window just to witness the return of the DLA man and his three pals. I pulled back the curtains only to observe a situation that would have ranked very highly in my Lancashire Constabulary days:

There appeared to be three on the mobility scooter and the remaining man pushing from behind. My first impression was; "The two extra ones on the scooter must intend signing on for the disability living allowance and are getting a bit of practise in on how to handle the little vehicle."
My next thought was; "If they keep this up there will be no need for a false claim – they will all be maimed."

That thought almost materialised for they tried to turn at ninety degrees from the pavement and into the scooter owner's flat. They crashed into the hand rail that had been erected to help the DLA man into his home, sending it scattering in pieces. All four would up in a great heap over the top of the little mobility scooter which was heaving and tugging as if trying to escape from the mass of drunkards on top of it. None of them seemed to have the slightest clue as to how to get out of the entanglement and unto their feet again. The wife whispered in my ear; "What would the police charge that lot with if they caught them?"
I shook my head; "Hard to say, for the offence of 'drunk in charge of a mobility scooter' would hardly stick as the wee scooter seems to be more aware of what's happened that all the others together.

As I mentioned before, when down-and-outs ask me for a couple of bob 'to buy a cup of tea' I always accompany my contribution to their demise with the words: "Now get yourself a pint and make sure not to waste that on a meal or something equally silly."

These unfortunates all have a tale, but it is one they no longer wish to tell and most of them have opted out of the system just to escape having to conform. Too many people make the mistake of assuming dishevelment and neglect equates to a lack of intelligence. Most of them have opted out in desperation and the last thing they want is patronisation.

Both my wife and I are interested in the welfare of birds and make sure they are supplied with an ample variety of seed which we hand up on a tree under the notice of: 'Tweet Shop.' Most of the seed winds up on the ground and from time to time strange plants sprout up amongst the flowers. One day our daughter-in-law asked: "Do you intend selling it or are you keeping it for personal use?"

"What," my wife asked?

"The weed."

"What weed?"

"The big cannabis plants you are growing in your front garden."
"Oh my good God," she gasped, "I thought they were flowers."
"You should hand them into the charity shop," the daughter-in-law laughed, "the sunshine bar people would pay good money for those."
They would up in the compost bin.

Recently, I was walking around an indoor market in Morecambe when I came across a religious stall that had many bibles, holy pictures and icons on display. There was a man there with a little engraving machine and he was prepared to inscribe any religious motto on whatever metal, artefacts one might chose to buy.
"Are you quite a religious person?" the man asked me.
"Oh very much so," I lied.
The wife anticipated what was to come and tried to tug me away.
"Would you like one of these little holy medallions here; they are very popular, Sir?"
The medals looked like bits of gold painted tin, so I asked: "Are these made from precious metal?"
"Semi-precious, Sir; semi-precious, Sir. What would you like inscribed on it?"

"Jesus Wept!"
The wife took me by the arm and shoved me away: "You don't half embarrass me. What are you trying to do?"
"Well, I was about to ask what he would charge for a second-hand 'Holy Grail' but you buggered it up."
"Get off! It's people like you that give us Irish a bad name."

My brothers, whom I fondly remember from our childhood days as: Teke and Jap grew up to be very good singers and musicians, and I feel proud that they decided to entertain old folk in homes through the Ards Peninsula in County Down. I went to hear them play in an old people's home in Portavogie where those who were awake clapped frequently then dozed off, those that were sleeping sometimes awoke and clapped enthusiastically just to drop back off with the others, whilst a couple of grumpy ones garbled sounds about: "Turning that radio down a bit." As we left I mentioned something about meeting up on the doorstep but Teke, keeping me right as he had done in childhood, pulled me back by the arm:

"What you said just now; it is taboo, you never say that in a place like this that is filled with people on the last stage of life:

"What did I say?"

"See you on the way out."

Typical Gorbals tenement block

A typical famine eviction around the time of Matilda's birth

Father and Mother with the first two items of potential trouble

Great Grandmother Matilda, Grandfather Patrick, Father Patrick, Self, Son Aaron, Granddaughter Beth

'Texas Sam'
Malachy

Cloughey Village in the forties. The patch of ground on the left is the Strifeacre. Note: Mister Keane arriving in his car. It has got to be Mister Keane as no one else owned a car in those days.

Mr Keane smoking

Mr Keane guarding

Mr Keane Posing

Kirkistown Castle where evolution was reversed and hens relearned how to fly

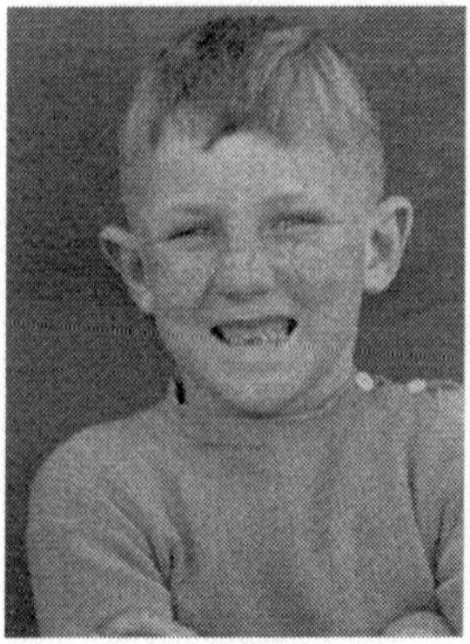

Flint who doubled as ammo runner and gun loader for the 'Hen Hurtler'

The raised second green at Kirkistown Golf club. Here and the similarly raised tenth green were the scenes where many a cunning plan was carried out and good-living golfers found themselves uttering superlatives not found in the New Testament

Sergeant 1853
Norman Potts

Little sisters: Yvonne, Mary and Joan (Wee Wong, Mazda and the Wane)

My big mate Dave Crobsbie and myself (inserted) outside Widnes old police station. They pulled it down a couple of years after my arrival.

Mount St Joseph, where our taxi careered out of control much to the embarassment of my mother and the joy of us young occupants

Where the two great bulls fought to the death - a horrendous duel that remained with me for the rest of my life

If the Wazer was driving the 'tough' miners picked a different bus

This is the scene of two drunken policemen from gallic nations having an early morning boxing match in full uniform

My son Aaron

My son Lee

My son Marcus

Cloughey Bay

The Worshipful Wazer

My wife Geraldine